The Hit Man's Dilemma

The Hit Man's Dilemma
Or, Business, Personal and Impersonal

Keith Hart

PRICKLY PARADIGM PRESS
CHICAGO

Prickly Paradigm Press, LLC
5629 South University Avenue
Chicago, Il 60637

www.prickly-paradigm.com

ISBN: 0-9728196-8-1
LCCN: 2005921572

Printed in the United States of America on acid-free
paper.

For Loula and Constance

Table of contents

"Don't take this personal, it's just business"

The Hit Man's Dilemma is about the tension between the impersonal conditions of social life and the persons who inevitably carry it out. This relationship is poorly understood, perhaps never more than now, when the difference between individual citizens and business corporations operating on a scale larger than some countries has become obscured. My starting point is a legendary remark made in a movie by a professional killer to his victim, "Don't take this personal, it's just business." But, according to my favorite American dictionary, a "person" is "a living human being" and what could be more personal than taking his life? Perhaps the hit man is referring to his own attitude, not to the effect. Killing people is a matter of routine for him, a "business" ("the occupation, work or trade in which a person is engaged"). Or there might still be an element of personal judgment involved, if his humanity is touched by the victim. More likely, an ethos of detachment makes the work easier, if at some emotional cost. Why should business be impersonal and, if it is, how can that be reconciled with the person who practices it?

Let's explore this tension a bit further. "Personal" is defined as "relating to a particular person, private; concerning a particular person's private business interests; aimed pointedly at the most intimate aspects of a person; relating to the body or physical being; (law) relating to movable property." So privacy seems to be intrinsic to whatever "personal" means, but what makes it particular can be either mental or physical and it seems to include rather than be opposed to business. "Private" in turn carries a freight of meaning: "secluded from the sight, presence or intrusion of others; intended for one's exclusive use; confined to the individual, personal; not available for public use, control or participation; belonging to a particular person, as opposed to the public; not for public knowledge or disclosure, secret; not appropriate for public display, intimate; placing a high value on personal privacy." To complete this round of definitions, someone or something is "particular" when they are "separate or distinct from others of the same category, group or nature." It is in the nature of persons to be particular, or, in Blake's words, "General Forms have their vitality in Particulars, and every Particular is a Man."

Apparently, keeping that distinctiveness poses problems for which privacy offers a potential solution. This is especially so when we are confronted by "the public" and, confusingly, by "business" also, even though it expresses "private" interests. Business is supposed to be "impersonal": "lacking personality, not being a person; showing no emotion; having no personal connection." But businesses can be persons too. In law, a "person" is "a human being or an organization with legal rights and duties." There are therefore real and artificial persons; and business corporations are the only organizations treated like individual citizens in economic law. Others such as churches and political parties, for instance, are not. And this right was won at a particular moment in history, the late nineteenth century. Since then, it has become more difficult to draw the line between living persons and abstract social entities that are much bigger and potentially longer-lasting than any human being. I will argue that our political and intellectual culture has become confused as a result, undermining the prospects for a genuine democracy and reinforcing rule by a remote oligarchy.

No wonder the hit man is muddled. Business is supposed to be impersonal despite being usually transacted between persons as an expression of their private interests. Worse, there is no difference in law between Walmart and you or me, so why shouldn't a killer claim impersonal reasons for inflicting bodily harm on another person? It's all in the mind, after all.

Ideas are impersonal, human life is not. So, at one level, the issue is the relative priority to be accorded to life and ideas. Because the encounter is live and therefore already personal, the hit man has to warn his victim (and perhaps himself) not to take it so. It would seem that the personal and the impersonal are hard to separate in practice. Our language and culture contain the ongoing history of this attempt to separate social life into two distinct spheres. This is the core of capitalism's moral economy; and gangster movies offer a vicarious opportunity to relive its contradictions. Here is a violent criminal claiming a detachment that would grace a bank manager. It is ludicrous, but then perhaps the two types of business are not as far apart as we are encouraged to think.

I will explore here the historical relationship between human personality and impersonal society, focusing on the institution of private property. This has somehow evolved in only a few centuries from being a source of personal autonomy in a citizen commonwealth to becoming the means whereby a few huge business corporations seek to dominate world economy. The question of money's role in society is obviously central to this; and indeed we will discover that the payment of money is often thought to render relations impersonal in capitalist societies. Meanwhile, property has shifted its main point of reference from things to ideas; having once been "real," it is now crucially "intellectual." This development is related to the revolution in digital communications that has begun to shrink our experience of distance in human relationships. For surely, what makes communication personal is when it takes place in the here and now, "face-to-face." But radical reductions in the cost of producing and transferring information through machines have injected a new dynamic into our relations, invoked by expressions like "virtual reality." And so the current crisis over "intellectual property" is closely linked to a transformation that is pulling society towards an increasingly global frame of reference. Modern corporations rely on extracting rents from property as much as on profits from direct sales; and, as the saying goes, "Information wants to be free," meaning that there is consistent downward pressure on prices for information-based goods and services. The social effort needed to maintain high prices in a world of increasingly free production and reproduction is what drives the conflict highlighted by this essay.

Business, especially of the hit man's kind, is always personal at one level and impersonal at another. The trick is to learn how to manage the tension between them. Moreover, his "business," the work of criminal gangs, is based on highly personal ties of loyalty to "families" and systematic resort to violence outside the law, in principle the opposite of the bureaucratic universe where most of us live and work. We know that modern business corporations have been granted the same legal status as living persons. And so, just as the gangster thinks of himself as a professional businessman, it turns out that corporations are quite capable of behaving like gangsters, with equal contempt for human life. This is not to claim that corporate executives are always criminals, just that the line between economic activities carried out within and outside the law is harder to draw in practice than their conventional separation would allow.

What the hit man would like his victim not to take personally is a contract, an impersonal act performed for money, but one intended to inflict personal injury. His business is violence, which is supposed to be the antithesis of modernity. The hit man is both modern and a relic of feudalism, of an age when men ruled in very personal ways through the threat of violence. Yet he cloaks himself in the language of "business." It is confusing, but then our times are confused. Maybe there is less difference between them and what came before than we would like to think. For this reason, Shakespeare, whose plays offer his extended reflections on the emergence of the Tudor state out of feudalism, has much to tell us about the awkward relationship between living persons and the impersonal offices they must fulfill.

The hit man's dilemma is to be or not to be human, whether or not to give an idea, "business," priority over life. So what does it take to be human? Rousseau claims in his *Second Discourse* (on inequality) that the two fundamental drives of human beings, which we share with the higher animals, are self-interest and compassion. The first says that each individual has a direct personal interest in self-preservation. The second is the Latin form for the Greek "sympathy" and its equivalent in Germanic English is "fellow feeling." He believed that our self-interest, a solitary quality, is moderated by an instinctive feeling of sympathy for others, mainly for others like ourselves, but also perhaps for all living creatures. He added a third human universal, the drive for self-improvement, and explained the progressive trend of history as its consequence.

So, from this perspective, we are isolated individuals who take part in societies that link us to the rest of humanity in one way or another. Each of us, in order to be human, must learn to be extraordinarily self-reliant. I call this the "toothbrush syndrome"— who will brush your teeth if not yourself? But writers in Rousseau's time lived with the pain that modern dental care has spared most of us. We also live in society and this requires us to learn to belong to others. This isn't easy, so that it often appears to us that the two principles are in conflict. Much of modern ideology emphasizes how hard it is to be individually self-interested and at the same time socially responsible, even compassionate, to be economic as well as social, we might say. Under these circumstances, when culture is set up to expect a conflict between the two, it is hard to be both. Yet the two sides are often inseparable in practice and some societies, by encouraging private and public interests to coincide, have managed to integrate them more effectively than ours. Our hit man does not live in one of these, however, since he must separate "business" from fellow feeling in his work.

At the heart of our public culture lies an impenetrable confusion. On the one hand we are taught to think of ourselves as distinctive personalities, on the other we are submerged in an abstract universe where people, things and ideas cannot be distinguished from each other. We no longer know how to act or in what context of mutual interdependence, since we either fail to connect with society or lose ourselves in it. The feminists were right to insist that the personal is political. The political too is often necessarily personal. But, if we relied on persons alone to make society, we would be back to feudalism or its modern equivalent, criminal mafias. There must be impersonal institutions that at least in principle work for everyone, regardless of who they are or who they know. But, as long as we remain trapped in a narrow concept of individual personality, the impersonal engines of society lie far beyond our grasp. What place is there for the humanity of individual persons in the dehumanized social frameworks we live by? This is the hit man's dilemma and it is ours too.

These are quite abstract issues, but they take on a more concrete significance in the historical context of the digital revolution and contemporary transformations of world economy. The task of building a democratic society where public institutions are conducive to personal freedom has been pushed by these developments to a more inclusive level. The fight is on to save the commons of human society, culture and ecology from the encroachments of corporate private property. This is no longer principally a question of conserving the earth's natural resources, although it is definitely that too, nor of the deterioration of public services left to the mercies of privatized agencies. The age of information has raised the significance of intangible commodities. Increasingly we buy and sell ideas; and their reproduction is made infinitely easier by digital technologies. So the larger corporations have launched a campaign to assert their exclusive ownership of what until recently might have been considered shared culture to which all had free and equal access. People who never knew they shared a common infrastructure of culture are now being forced to acknowledge it by aggressive policies of corporate privatization. Across the board, separate battles are being fought, without any real sense of the common cause that they embody:

1. *Music.* File-sharing of popular music, harbinger of peer-to-peer exchange between individual computers, pits the feudal barons of the music business against our common right to transmit songs as we wish.

2. *The moving image.* The world of film, television and video is likewise a site of struggle sharpened by fast-breaking technologies affecting their distribution and use.

3. *Language, literature and law.* In many ways, our ability to draw freely on a common heritage is being undermined by the aggressive assertion of copyright, as in the reproduction of case law or the claim of copyright in normal words by businesses.

4. *The internet.* What began as a free communications network for a scientific minority is now the contested domain of giant corporations, governments and an army of hackers.

5. *Software.* The free software and open source movement, setting Linux and the said army of hackers against Microsoft's monopoly, has opened up fissures within corporate capitalism itself.

6. *GMOs.* The shift to manufactured food varieties linked to proprietary chemicals and seeds has introduced a similar struggle to agriculture in the context of growing public concern about genetic modification.

7. *Pharmaceuticals.* The big drugs companies try to ward off the threat posed to their lucrative monopolies by cheap generics aimed at the Third World populations who need them most.

8. *The universities.* As the home environment for the bulk of the intellectuals whose rights are allegedly at stake, academic culture itself has undergone a shift from communal sharing to private ownership of ideas.

This general conflict has its specific origin in the 1860s and subsequent decades, when the liberal revolutions of the seventeenth to mid-nineteenth centuries gave way in the leading industrial countries to a system of national capitalism, the management of accumulation and markets by central bureaucracies. Faced with unruly urban populations, big money made an alliance with the traditional ruling classes to secure unequal contracts between owners and workers, sellers and buyers, lenders and borrowers. The problem then and now is, how do you make people pay up? New legal frameworks were devised granting to corporations both limited liability and the private property rights of individual citizens. In its heyday, national capitalism was able to police this confusing situation in the interests of large-scale bureaucracy. But developments in the last quarter-century, leading to the emergence of powerful transnational actors, have made this increasingly difficult. That is why we are now witnessing what might otherwise seem absurd corporate encroachments on public culture.

The crux of the matter is the shift from an eighteenth century moral politics of persons acting within institutional frameworks (as envisaged by the writers of the United States Constitution) to one where personal and impersonal agency have been merged, to the detriment of our ability to distinguish between living individuals and abstract social entities. The place of morality in public life inevitably suffers when personal responsibility is overshadowed by impersonal interests. This is the metaphysical ground for politicians to be widely perceived as immoral and bureaucrats as inhumane. The result is rising lawlessness and imperialism, even fascism, on the part of transnational corporations and national governments taking their lead from Bush's USA. Effective resistance to privatization of the cultural commons requires us to build a public space where personal morality and universal human interests can find common ground. If we wish to understand the obstacles such a project would face, we must revisit the entire modern history of capitalism. There is a geographical dimension to this history too. World production is now being relocated in Asia, while control of global economic institutions remains firmly in the hands of the West. The culmination of national capitalism in increasingly strident attempts to control the "neo-liberal" world economy from America and Europe coincides with the most significant shift in economic power since Germany and the United States challenged British hegemony over a century ago.

The hit man's dilemma is a metaphor for the moral problems inherent in building modern society on the basis of impersonal institutions. This leads to a division between personal agency and the impersonal conditions of that agency that is hard to sustain. I begin the main body of the essay with the anomalous relationship between morality and politics, law or business, as we encounter it in works of fiction, especially in movies and plays. Here I juxtapose West and East, gangster flicks from Hollywood and Bollywood, historical tragedies by Shakespeare and Kurosawa, to show the universal contradiction between the conduct of public institutions and the living persons who embody them. Next, I approach the problem through the modern history of impersonal society, starting with the attempt to construct separate spheres of personal and impersonal relations in capitalist economies, then taking in bureaucracy and scientific knowledge. This leads to a short account of private property from its modern origins in the liberal revolutions of seventeenth-century England to the instrument of corporate global domination it has become today, focusing on the confusion that arises from the collapse of the legal distinction between living persons and business corporations. This is related to the process whereby the struggle for control of economic value has moved from one over land and labor to "intellectual" property.

Our moment in history is defined by the digital revolution in communications which, in speeding up the formation of world society as a single interactive network, has introduced a new dimension to personal and impersonal culture, "virtual reality." The result is the world war launched by transnational corporations, with the full complicity of the USA and other governments, to privatize the cultural commons. The idea of "intellectual property," referring to copyright, patents and trademarks, lends a spurious conceptual unity to what might more accurately be described as "information feudalism." This attempt to establish a new kind of global command economy uses technologies that are inherently progressive and revolutionary. Nor is it the first time that corporate monopoly has been undermined by the restless forces of innovation. The American movie industry was located in Hollywood a century ago as a way of evading the restrictions imposed by Edison's east coast monopoly. Now it seeks to impose its own monopoly on the "piracy" rampant in Asia and elsewhere. The shift in world production from West to East will only be accelerated if western governments grant their corporations the rigid controls they seek. Finally, I reprise the pamphlet that launched Prickly Paradigm's predecessor imprint in examining the crisis of the universities and of intellectuals in general. For our problem is to learn to think clearly as much as to act effectively. How is democracy attainable unless each of us can find moral grounds for personal judgment in a world driven by impersonal forces that we can never fully understand? What is at stake here is the need for a new humanism that meets the measure of our common humanity. In this version, people must work through the institutions of money and machines, not against them.

The moral dilemma in politics, law and business

Morality concerns the principles of good behavior, what we ought to do. We all want to be good and would usually like others to see us that way. Although it is possible to express "the good" abstractly as a rule—"always be kind to children and animals"—morality can only be expected of persons who face the choice to be good or otherwise in complex situations that cannot be reduced to simple rules. Moreover, these actions are not isolated, but build up over time to form an impression of good character or its opposite. What politics, law and business have in common is that they define "the good" in a collective sense. A group must be protected from subversion, disorder or loss and this more general good may require leaders in particular to sacrifice personal morality to that impersonal end. For some purposes, the exercise of effective power alone will suffice. But it costs too much if people must always be forced to do what you want. It helps if they can be persuaded to do something because they believe it is right. Often that means believing that a leader is a good person. It is not easy in practice to separate the impersonal ends of society from their personal instruments.

When society is organized through depersonalized rules, as ours has been for a century or more, the normative exclusion of personal judgment as a force for good or evil generates a permanent moral crisis. It is hard to discuss this crisis using the methods of impersonal social science, although that hasn't stopped some from trying. Here I will draw principally on works of fiction, especially movies, since they are designed to give dramatic expression to this very question. But I will also refer to Max Weber's historical sociology, since it hinges on the same issue. As a change of pace from Italian gangster movies, I start with *Company* (2002), an Indian film about organized crime in Mumbai. Since a minor theme of this essay is that world economy is shifting inexorably from West to East, an example taken from Bollywood's prolific output is appropriate.

Mallik becomes the acknowledged leader of Mumbai's equivalent of "the outfit" in Chicago by killing off his principal rivals in a series of brutal putsches. He selects a young outsider, Chandu, as a lieutenant and promotes him as their faction wins centralized control of this violent business. At one stage the gang goes offshore, operating from Hong Kong and other Asian cities. Throughout the movie face-to-face encounters are mediated by conversations at distance using cell phones. If the railway locomotive was the symbol of nineteenth-century industrial capitalism, the symbol of virtual capitalism in our day is the mobile phone. The Company goes international largely through use of this new technology: "The telephone became the biggest weapon in the underworld." A dazzling scene consists of a rapid montage of city landscapes with a soundtrack of phones ringing.

The political crisis comes when Mallik, operating from a distance, tries to limit his reliance on Chandu. Having plucked him from nowhere, he feels he has become too dependent on the young man and transfers some of his power to Krishnan, another lieutenant. There is friction on the ground as a result and Mallik responds to it by having Chandu's friend killed because he couldn't get along with Krishnan. This naturally weakens his moral authority over Chandu, but the latter remains overtly loyal. Then Mallik delegates a hit to Chandu, the assassination of a politician, that he decides to abort for operational reasons. This is the last straw for Mallik who moves swiftly to have Chandu killed; but, thanks to the friendship of their women and the mobile phone, he escapes and civil war breaks out, spreading as far as Nairobi in Kenya. The resulting mayhem fragments the Company and lends strength to their enemies, including the police. Chandu eventually surrenders to the authorities in order to give evidence against Mallik and this phase of organized crime in Mumbai is effectively over.

Everything hinges on the personal relationship between the two leading men. Mallik is a political realist ("friendship lasts as long as it lasts") who understands what he takes to be human universals better than those who prefer not to recognize them. His girlfriend says "You're really a Satan" and he says "There's a Satan in everyone." Elsewhere she reflects, "Sometimes I think there's a monster hidden in you." "There's a monster in every human being. It's just that some people are scared of confronting it." Our capacity to treat human beings impersonally, in the last resort to kill them with indifference, is part of the human condition, but we deny this. He has learned to live with it better than most and that makes him faster to strike when he has to.

Chandu is younger and less ruthless. He justifies his way of life as the only chance he had to prosper: "no-one can make it to the top the right way." He has not given up on the idea of being a moral person or of judging others by their personal merits. Thus he thinks Raote, the politician who commissions the assassination of a minister in order to succeed him, is "not a proper guy." One of the weaker soldiers thinks this is funny, since it reveals Chandu to be a criminal who believes there is honor among thieves. But of course it is also his strength as a rising leader that he hasn't abandoned the notion of right. This leads him to baulk at killing the children of the minister when they join him in the car that is to be blown up. He calls off the hit unilaterally. When sanctioned for insubordination, he says "If the Company can do without me, I can do without the Company." And that is that, as far as Mallik is concerned. When, towards the end, Mallik is blamed for what everyone now realizes was a mistake, someone says, "Whatever's happening is the fault of the business, not one man." But, of course, this business can only operate with one big boss or it fragments into impotence, as now. After the terrible dénouement, Chandu hands himself over to the state and tries to make it up with Mallik. "I am about to do what I think is right. If you suffer any losses, don't take it personally." Don't take this personal, it's just business. But actually it is Chandu's attempt to salvage morality from the mess. The hit man's dilemma is between morality and politics. Morality is always personal and the warfare of criminal enterprise is inevitably impersonal. (One of the theme tunes at key moments is "Mars" from Holst's *The Planets*). Chandu embodies the contradiction more than the rest. He is a classic individualist, in a long line of American westerns and comic strips of the *Dick Tracy* genre, the loner who doesn't believe in justice unless he does it himself. He legitimates his own choices by judging official society to be as corrupt as he is, but less honest; and in any case the game is stitched up to exclude him. Another precursor is the rootless young intellectual, Raskolnikov in Dostoevsky's *Crime and Punishment*, who believes that "if someone would do anything new, he must be a criminal." He is the prototype of today's teenage hackers for whom breaking the rules is the point of their inventiveness. Like Raskolnikov and his nemesis, the detective Porphyry, Chandu meets his match in the clever and basically decent policeman, Sreenivasan. The latter knows the police can't be effective if they always stay within the law. The law doesn't measure up, but it is all we have if we are not to be subject to rule by the mob. And Chandu's catharsis comes from killing Raote, when the minister visits his cell in order to tell him to shut up. The lines between official politics, the law and crime are blurred in practice, even if the public prefers to believe in their fundamental separateness.

Having scored a victory that leaves many issues unresolved, Sreenivasan retires to be head of a police training college and is said to be writing a novel based on his experiences with the underworld, called *Company*... In the meantime, he is the film's voiceover who says things like "The Company stands on one thing. That's fear." It was built with "three weapons — murder, money and compromise." One recurrent jingle in the background chants in Hindi "Yes, it stinks, but it's business." The appeal of gangster movies is that they allow us to see society from a position outside the self-protective cocoon of law, bureaucracy and normal business that the middle classes inhabit. More subversively, by drawing on the language and imagery of normal capitalism, the gangster "firm" offers a metaphor for the dark side of the age of money in which we all live. Tony Soprano crosses the thin line between hoodlum and suburbanite many times every day. That's why HBO's *The Sopranos* is so successful. Impersonal society in its official guise can be just as immoral as criminal enterprise, except that thieves have personal lives based on morality of a sort and universal rules have no room for morality at all.

As in *King Lear*, the women play a key role in the unfolding of *Company*'s drama. When the conflict between one-man rule and the personal morality of his chief henchman provokes bloody civil war and mutual destruction, they offer humane resistance to the logic of "kill or be killed." Like any great tragedy, this series of human catastrophes hinges on an objective contradiction, the one Max Weber identified with patrimonial bureaucracy. The origins of impersonal government lie in the king's use of palace organization to assert his independence from the feudal barons who control the bulk of the people in the countryside. He needs a staff and recruits them as individuals who owe allegiance solely to him. But there is always the problem of distance, since officials are pulled towards asserting their own independence of him by their reliance on local resources. Beyond that he can't afford to let any of his henchmen get too big in case they try to take his place. Relatively stable forms of patrimonial bureaucracy depend on working out institutional rules for checking this tendency, such as moving officials around so that they can't develop local attachments or hiving off part of the job as a way of undermining a potential rival. This structural contradiction underlies conflicts whose instruments are the personal actors.

The best dramatic example of Weber's analysis I know is Eisenstein's *Ivan the Terrible Part 1*, where the Tsar takes on the feudal boyars with the aid of a patrimonial staff and finally gets the people to beg him to be their absolute monarch. But *Company* is a pretty good instance too, as are most of Shakespeare's history plays and tragedies. These often hinge on the tension between human personality and impersonal institutions. How can a holder of high office reconcile his public role with being just a man? Is it possible to move beyond kingship and mob rule to a genuinely democratic society? His Elizabethan audiences sat on the edges of their seats, knowing that the future of their own Tudor state was at stake in the drama. When Hamlet asks "To be or not to be?" his ambivalent attachment to life also evokes the fundamental contradiction that requires some people to be human and inhuman, personal and depersonalized at once or in quick succession. This is a political question, but it has often been seen as merely existential and narcissistic in Hamlet's case. If feudalism was a mess and basically unjust, what is the role for human personality in a more equal and universal social system? Shakespeare, in the course of writing all his plays, dug deeper into this core issue of modern politics than anyone has since.

Shakespeare was far from being a revolutionary—he became a country gentleman and leaned politically to an aristocratic faction. But the question he pursued in his "Wars of the Roses" plays, from Bolingbroke's usurpation of the monarchy to Henry Tudor's victory at Bosworth Field, also drove his greatest tragedies—what are the human consequences of centralizing society as a single agency embodied in just one man? The evidence of the last and greatest of his tragedies, *King Lear*, is bleak indeed, since the answer seems to be that monarchy ends in madness and civil war. Modern audiences usually miss the point about Shakespeare's political plays, focusing on the psychological drama while neglecting the problem of social structure. In classical Aristotelian fashion, the plays often open with a rupture of the social order: the state of Denmark is out of joint and in a general moral crisis. The personal drama unfolds, but the end of the play is the restoration of political order: Fortinbras turns up in Act IV to put things straight. The film version of *Julius Caesar* (1953) left out Act IV altogether, the formation of the empire following Octavian's victory in the civil war, since Hollywood movies, like the press and TV, deal in personalities, not social history.

Yet occasionally a journalist recognizes the relevance of Shakespeare's theme for modern politics. Nicholas D. Kristof wrote an op-ed piece in the *New York Times* on the eve of the presidential election, "Crowning Prince George" (1 September 2004) that drew an analogy between George W. Bush and Prince Hal/Henry V. The lesson Kristof draws from Shakespeare's plays is "that the world is full of nuances and uncertainties, and that leaders self-destruct when they are too rigid, too sure of themselves or too intoxicated by moral clarity." He also cites the bard to point to the larger human contradictions of politics and war:

> But if the cause be not good, the king himself
> hath a heavy reckoning to make when all those legs

and arms and heads chopped off in a battle shall
join together at the latter day and cry all "We died
at such and such a place," some swearing, some
crying for a surgeon, some upon their wives left
poor behind them, some upon the debts they owe,
some upon their children rawly left. I am afeared
there are few die well that die in a battle.

The columnist leaves this reader wondering
how it comes about that a play concerned with feudal
thugs is so relevant to the leadership of the modern
world's greatest democracy.

To insist on Shakespeare's universality as an
interpreter of modern history and the general human
condition could be said to be a typical western exag-
geration. For this reason, Kurosawa's movies about
medieval and early modern Japan offer a valuable
extension of the cultural range. *Kagemusha* (1980)
translates as "the shadow of the warrior." Here too the
question is, What happens when the destiny of society
is entrusted to a few individuals? Kurosawa uses the
notion of a double to highlight the contrast between
high office and its personal incumbent. A great lord
dies at a critical point in a war with rival clans and a
thief who looks just like him is recruited to play his
part. The double is a miserable specimen of humanity,
but he has some native wit and learns the role.
Women and children are the most difficult to
convince because they are less impressed by social
appearances. The period is the Japanese equivalent of
England's War of the Roses, the transition from
feudalism to the beginnings of the modern state. The

losing side in this case is the one that tries the subterfuge of the double. The winning side and founder of the Japanese state is the Tokugawa clan. The climactic battle symbolizes the passage from traditional to modern warfare, as the horses of the losers are mown down by fusillades of gunfire. The credits at the end of the film run over the corpse of the double as it floats downstream, where it crosses a submerged flag whose abstract symbolism shows us which aspects of feudalism the modern state will borrow. Personality is vanquished. One striking feature of the movie is the persistent strong breeze ripping through the banners, a symbol of the winds of change running through sixteenth century Japan at much the same time that Shakespeare wrote his plays.

It is conventional to treat this dawn of modernity in the West and East as having been superceded by the impersonal society it gave rise to. This was certainly Max Weber's view. He saw no end to a disenchanted world devoid of meaning and personality where the iron cage of modern rational structures squeezes the life out of us all and subordinates us to dehumanized institutions — bureaucracy, the market, science. I beg to differ. The world has changed less than we sometimes think and the dialectic of personal and impersonal agency is just as strong now as it was then. Stories about gangsters, both medieval and modern, remind us that the moral dilemmas of political life have not gone away. Against the pessimism of Shakespeare and Weber, we can still seek new solutions to the hit man's dilemma.

Impersonal society as a modern project

The twentieth century was built on a universal social experiment. Society was conceived of as an impersonal mechanism defined by international division of labor, national bureaucracy and scientific laws understood only by experts. Not surprisingly, most people feel ignorant and impotent in the face of such a society. Yet, we have never been more conscious of ourselves as unique personalities who make a difference. And we are only too ready to grant our political leaders the ability to control the anonymous forces of society that lie beyond our own grasp. Moreover, even if the rules are impersonal, actual social organization consists of real people doing things to and with each other. Consequently we experience society as personal and impersonal at once, despite the huge cultural effort that goes into separating the two. "Business" lies at the heart of the matter, for division of the economy into impersonal and personal spheres is capitalism's modern project for us all.

The hit man lives in a society where normal business often requires the suspension of ordinary humanity. An action may be objectively rational, but the victim is likely to feel hurt. Sacking an employee, calling in a loan or evicting a tenant, whatever the cause, may end up as a personal conflict. When confronted as a source of personal injury, the perpetrator retreats behind the organization's rules as just the carrier of the message, an instrument of economic logic, "the bottom line." Partly because of this, we are taught to imagine that the payment of money makes a huge difference to a transaction's social significance. It is not so in most of the world's societies. I was once talking to a Ghanaian student about exchanges between lovers in his country and he said that it was common there for a boy, after sleeping with a girl he has met at a party, to leave some money as a gift and token of esteem. He had once done this with a visiting American student and the resulting explosion was gigantic: "Do you imagine that I am a prostitute?" and so on. Where does that moral outrage come from? Why does money matter so much to us?

Buying and selling human beings is an old practice. We call it slavery. A wage, however, is a pledge, a promise to pay when the work is done, which is more flexible than slavery and ties up much less capital. A flood of rural-urban migrants into industrial employment established wage labour as the norm in nineteenth-century Europe. This led to an attempt to separate the spheres in which paid and unpaid work predominated. The first was ideally objective and impersonal, specialised and calculated; the second was subjective and personal, diffuse, based on long-term interdependence. Inevitably, the one was associated with the payment of money in a public place or "business," the other with "home;" so that "work" usually meant outside activities, and maintaining families became known as "housework." Now we earn money when we work and we spend it in our spare time, which is focused on the home, so that production and consumption are linked in an endless cycle. But it is not easy. Especially at times of crisis, it is difficult to keep the personal and the impersonal apart; yet our economic culture demands nothing less of us.

One sphere is a zone of infinite scope where things, and increasingly human creativity, are bought and sold for money, the market. The second is a protected sphere of domestic life, where intimate personal relations hold sway, home. The market is unbounded and, in a sense, unknowable, whereas the bounds of domestic life are known only too well. The normal link between the two is that some adults, traditionally men more than women, go out to work, to "make" the money on which the household subsists. The economy of the home rests on spending this money and performing services without payment. The result is a heightened sense of division between an outside world where our humanity feels swamped and a precarious zone of protected personality at home. This duality is the moral and practical foundation of capitalist society and prostitution exposes its contradictions. What could be more personal than sex and more impersonal than a money payment?

The attempt to construct a market where commodities are exchanged instantly and impersonally as alienable private property is utopian. The idea of civil society in this sense was to grant a measure of independence for businesses from the arbitrary interventions of rulers. All the efforts of economists to insist on the autonomy of market logic cannot disguise the fact that businesses and market relations more generally have a personal and social component, particularly when the commodity being bought and sold is human creativity. Until not long ago, markets and money were minor appendages of agricultural society, largely external to relations that organised the performance of work and the distribution of its product. The middle-class revolution of the seventeenth and eighteenth centuries prepared the way for markets to be accepted at the centre of society. But the industrial revolution made selling one's labour for wages the main source of livelihood. Only now did the market for human services become the main means of connecting families to society.

Where does the social pressure come from to make business impersonal? Weber had one answer: rational calculation of profit in enterprises depends on the capitalist's ability to control product and factor markets, especially that for labor. But human work is not an object separable from the person performing it, so people must be taught to submit to the impersonal disciplines of the workplace. To some extent, this insistence on impersonal rules is just an ideology. As every participant knows, businesses consist of relations between persons. But the forms of bureaucracy also impose their own reality on economic life. The war to impose these rules has never been completely won. So, just as money is intrinsic to the home economy, personality remains intrinsic to the workplace, which means that the cultural effort required to keep the two spheres separate, if only at the conceptual level, is huge. We, who have submitted to this confusing paradigm of division, often accuse others of backwardness for refusing to acknowledge its force. The word we use is "corruption." But, as Chandu insisted, the rhetoric that separates formal organization from informal practice might well be less honest than an open acknowledgment of their interdependence.

Money in capitalist societies stands for alienation, detachment, impersonal society, the outside; its origins lie beyond our control. Relations marked by the absence of money are the model of personal integration and free association, of what we take to be familiar, the inside. Commodities are "goods" because we consume them in person, but we find it difficult to embrace money, the means of their exchange, as "good" because it belongs to a sphere that is indifferent to morality and, in some sense, stays there. The good life, instead of uniting work and home, is restricted to what takes place in the latter. This institutional dualism, forcing individuals to divide themselves, asks too much of us. People want to integrate division, to make some meaningful connection between themselves as subjects and society as an object. It helps that money, as well as being the means of separating public and domestic life, was always the main bridge between the two. That is why money must be central to any attempt to humanize society. Today it is both the principal source of our vulnerability in society and the main practical symbol allowing each of us to make an impersonal world meaningful. If Emile Durkheim said we worship society and call it God, then money is the God of capitalist society.

Many people would sign up for the notion that money is the root of all evil. But, in demonizing money, they come close to endowing the institution with power all of its own. Karl Marx wrote in *Capital* about "the fetishism of commodities and the secret thereof." The word fetiche is Portuguese for a West African custom of dedicating a shrine to a spirit that is thought to inhabit a particular place. So, if you need to swim across a dangerous river, a sacrifice to the spirit of the river will help you succeed. Marx considered this to be an example of religious alienation. In his view the spirit was an invention of the human mind; but the Africans experienced their own creation as a superior agency capable of granting life or death. Something similar, he believed, was at work in our common attitudes to markets and money. Commodities are things made by people; money is the means we have created for facilitating their exchange. Yet we often experience markets as animated objects exercising a power over us that is devoid of human content, a force usually manifested in the money form. Prices go up and down, more often up, in a way that undermines our ability to manage our own lives. Marx thought we might overcome this alienation since, unlike the spirits produced by religious imagination, we know that human labour is the source of the commodities we exchange for money. *Capital* was designed to show the way towards such an emancipation.

We want to believe that the money we live by at least has a secure objective foundation. Georg Simmel thought of society as an endlessly proliferating network of exchanges (in other words, a market). He rejected the British attempt to base money on the objective certainty of a gold standard, since this reinforced a notion of money as something outside our individual or collective control. He saw it rather as a symbol of our interdependence, locating its value in the trust that comes from membership in society. Like Marx, he identified a parallel between the abstraction of money prices in commodity exchange and the abstraction of thought (scientific analysis) that represents the highest level of our cognitive interaction with the world.

For Simmel, there is no objective truth, no absolute on which we can hang our faith in existence. All we have are the subjective judgments we have made over time. Truth is relative to its application. Similarly, the value of commodities is not based on some objective standard, but is merely the outcome of what people are willing to pay in relation to all the other goods and services they want, given the resources at their disposal. Money is the means of making these complex calculations. This was roughly the position of the new marginalist economics of the day. So money is the common measure of value uniting all the independent acts of exchange, stabilizing the volatile world of commodity exchange, much as Durkheim thought society lent stability to the fluctuations of everyday life. Money, of course, is itself relative; but Simmel thought it represents an element of coherence in a world of constantly shifting prices. We are not yet ready to face the complex relativity of the real world, and so take comfort from money's symbolic steadiness. Most people prefer to believe that there is something out there we can rely on. If God is dead and Society has been killed off by the economists, then let Money be something real and enduring.

The engine of a capitalist economy is thus the alternation of citizens between production for wages outside the home and consumption within it using both money earnings and unpaid labor. This state of affairs was arrived at with much difficulty and then only partially, since such a division is not normal in human societies, where public affairs (including commerce) are generally carried out by individuals acting in their personal capacity. It rests on a gap between ideas and life that remains a tremendous cultural obstacle to the establishment of meaningful morality at the core of our common affairs. A similar attempt to found politics and administration on impersonal principles was also central to modern democracy. Feudalism identified society with a few privileged individuals, ultimately with the person of the emperor, the king, the bishop or the local lord, depending on political scale. Their approval was necessary if anything was to be done. The city states of the Italian Renaissance and then the emergent nation-states of Europe, especially England, sought to devise public institutions whose benefits were guaranteed equally to all, regardless of who they were or whom they knew. These bureaucracies had their origin in the palace staffs of patrimonial rulers; but they aimed at a new kind of universal democracy.

Weber tackled the problem of personal meaning in an impersonal society in his essay, *The City: on non-legitimate domination*. His was also an era of globalization and mass movement, the decades around 1900, when 50 million Europeans left home for the temperate lands of new settlement and the same number of Asian "coolies" were shipped to the tropical colonies. Western imperial rivalries culminated in the First World War; a vastly increased urban workforce was threatening socialist revolution; and the lines of political society were more fluid than ever before. So what did Weber mean by this typically awkward expression "non-legitimate domination'? He believed that society everywhere is held together by force. But always having to beat people over the head to make them comply is expensive. Better by far to persuade them that your political authority is based on right ("legitimate"). All rulers claim that their power is legitimate and the form of that claim to moral leadership affects how they exercise it. Thus, if the king governs by divine right, he should not arrange for the head of his church to be killed. Weber went on to observe that morality is a property of relations between persons, so that the exercise of power as a right (legitimate domination) was traditionally bound up with the persons of rulers and ruled. The ideas supporting a political system might be impersonal, but they were embodied in relations between actual human beings. This had its downside: getting what you wanted in such a "feudal" society depended on a highly unequal personalized hierarchy in which most people didn't count at all.

The Italian cities tried to break with this limitation on society. They wanted citizens to be equal before the law and rights and duties to be distributed in society according to universal principles. This democratic movement found expression in new institutional forms: the idea of the "people;" the university; state bureaucracy; and businesses oriented to the mass market. Weber termed this "rational-legal domination," rule according to impersonal principles whose justification is the abstract common good, as determined by law and the exercise of objective reason. There is no room for the morality of persons in such a system. If you go to city hall to complain about your local tax bill, it is inappropriate to get upset with the official you encounter there. It is not her fault. First, check what it says in the record and have the general reasons for it explained. If you are still unhappy, go find your political representative. For the system also depends on keeping politics and administration notionally separate. There is a lot to be said for the equity and efficiency of such a depersonalized system. But Weber noted two drawbacks. First, bureaucrats tend to accumulate unaccountable power that can be used against the people they claim to serve; and in this he anticipated Stalin. Second, the absence of a moral basis for rule (related to the increased marginality of religion) generates a crisis of legitimacy that can only be filled by charismatic leaders; and in this way he predicted the rise of Hitler.

If modern society is impersonal to a significant degree, then this aspect of our common existence is symbolized by the state. The state is society centralized as a single agency and traditionally this has been embodied in one person, the monarch or latterly the president. Shakespeare's tragedies trace out the implications of this and, as we have seen, he concluded in the last of them, *King Lear*, that such an arrangement is potentially disastrous. Even so, a strong element of personal rule persists in representative democracies. Indeed their legitimacy still sometimes rests on hereditary monarchs. The path from representative democracy to non-elective oligarchy and dictatorship remains a short one. Some philosophers have argued that the embodiment of the state in a concrete person is essential, that human beings cannot be governed by an entity devoid of personality. An analogous convergence of personal and impersonal organization took place in the economy. Capitalism came to depend from the second half of the nineteenth century on regulation of markets and money by national bureaucracies; and mass production for national and world markets entailed the rise of a management hierarchy within the capitalist enterprises themselves. Although corporations were a long-established feature of mercantile empire, something new occurred when businesses were simultaneously accorded the rights of individual citizens and excused some of their responsibilities, such as personal liability for bad debts. When corporations became legal persons sheltering their owners behind impersonal privilege, the drive to separate personal and impersonal spheres of economic life was reversed. Our political and intellectual culture has not yet recovered from the resulting confusion.

If feudalism was a mess and basically unjust, what is the role for human personality in a more equal and universal social system? Modern gangster movies allow us to approach this question metaphorically. Criminal mafias operate on a quasi-feudal basis, combining strong personal ties with violent behavior outside the law. Yet they exist in a world of modern states, bureaucracy and capitalist markets. No wonder the hit man is confused. What he is about to do is deeply personal—what could affect an individual more than being disfigured or killed? But the killer must be detached from the human consequences of his actions. He is just following orders issued in the name of the impersonal rules that sustain their common "business." We are appalled and intrigued by the story since it offers an extreme commentary on our own experience of daily life. The hit man's dilemma is ours too.

Along with these developments in economic and political life, something similar eventually took root in the transmission of knowledge. In late eighteenth century England, "experience" and "experiment" meant much the same thing; but before long the first came to mean the haphazard lessons that you and I derive from what happens to us and the second referred to the systematic basis for scientific knowledge acquired by experts. In this way personal and impersonal knowledge were separated on the grounds of being subjective and objective, particular and universal respectively. Education became the process of imparting standard knowledge gained without reference to personal experience. A branch that recognized the importance of individual persons in knowledge production was retained under the rubric of the "arts" or "humanities;" but the dominant means of controlling nature and society were the sciences. In theory a prerequisite for gaining such scientific knowledge was detachment from the object of enquiry. Intellectuals had always elevated general ideas and the books that contained them above personal experience. The precursor of secular ideology was after all organized religion. But this process went so far as to abolish people even from the disciplines that claimed to study them. It is not surprising that the word "don" means both mafioso and academic, for they both live by dehumanizing themselves and others. Violence is always there, just beneath the surface, as the following story shows.

It was the first decade of the nineteenth century in the small university town of Jena and the students were revolting. Napoleon's proletarian armies had already smashed the antiquated political structures of a fragmented Germany. One day a student took a pistol along to his lectures and shot the professor dead. On being arrested, he gave as his defense Kant's categorical imperative. A decade or two before, with the world opening up under the impetus of the French revolution, British industry and the international movement to abolish slavery, Immanuel Kant asked how the peoples of the world might find a way of living together beyond the reach of territorial states. He concluded that everyone wants to be good, even if what passes for being good varies between cultures; and that universal idea provided humanity with a framework for a conversation about making a just society. This moral premise—the categorical imperative to be ethical in one's dealings with others or, in its Christian form, to do unto others as we would have them do unto us— provided a basis for constructing society where the writ of state-made laws no longer operated. Kant's moral politics was the apogee of the liberal Enlightenment, an attempt to found civil society on the personal judgment of self-reliant individuals, and the student in question used this to explain what he had done. The German states were in disarray and each citizen of the world had to base his actions on universal morality, not on the ineffective laws of corrupt states. If he himself were ever guilty of poisoning the minds of the young with pernicious rubbish, then he too would deserve to die. It was his duty to do good by eradicating evil.

The prosecution called as an expert witness the university's rector, G.W.F. Hegel, the greatest German philosopher of his day. We can imagine the local audience waiting to hear his testimony with bated breath—would he try to appease the students or side with the old regime? Hegel just said:

No self-respecting community can allow its members to go around killing whoever they like. Kant's moral politics were the last dying gasp of bourgeois individualism, a failed attempt to make society on the basis of contract-bearing persons. The philosopher's task is to help us understand the movement of societies in history and to devise states that work better for their members. The proper object of philosophy is society, not the individual; and it is the university's job to train a class of professional experts capable of running the state in the interest of all. It is not enough to want to be good. We must be held accountable for the social consequences of our actions and murder is a crime against the community. Ideally citizens will come to recognize the laws as being in their own interest and then public life will be ethical.

In other words, if a child breaks a plate and tearfully says "I didn't mean to," Hegel would say "If you meant to, you would be a monster; but, in order to live with others, we learn how to avoid harming them, for instance, by being careful not to break their plates." We have to live in societies whose principles have an impersonal validity. The question then becomes how and why do those principles move in history? Like his contemporaries David Ricardo and Auguste Comte, he was inventing systematic social science.

There is only one word for law in English, but two in most other European languages. The English common-law tradition, exported most notably to America and other colonies, conceives of the public sphere as an extension of private relations between individuals. For this reason, Britain still lacks a written constitution and law is made to a large extent on the basis of judicial precedent. In origin the "individuals" concerned were feudal barons seeking to limit the independent authority of the king (as in the famous Magna Carta)—the little people were invisible. But this legal culture allowed England during the seventeenth century to take the lead in establishing a "civil society" whose economic interests were increasingly independent of the state. Owners of enterprises acquired property rights that were not extended to their workers, who were then generally known as "servants." Democracy is always relative. European law, on the other hand, is divided more clearly into two separate spheres—public law is handed down by the state and private right belongs to individuals. Hence, following Roman *ius* and *lex*, we find the pairs *droit* and *loi*, *Recht* and *Gesetz*, etc. Of course, national differences are more blurred than this contrast would suggest; but it is relevant to the degree of separation of personal and impersonal spheres. The attempt to separate public and private domains runs up against deeper cultural resistance in the English-speaking societies that have had the most to do with the development of capitalism to its present global level.

By the mid-twentieth century, what began as a social experiment in some small Italian cities, had become a war for control of world society between varieties of bureaucratic state—fascism, communism and welfare state democracy. The nuclear nightmare of the Cold War only intensified feelings of powerlessness among ordinary people who had long ago lost the ability to comprehend their societies in terms that were personally meaningful. People, machines and money are what matter in this world, in that order. But the first industrial revolution led Marx to observe that the order of precedence in Victorian society was the opposite, with human work, conceived of as an abstract category, labor, now reduced to tending machines in factory production; while the whole process was controlled by money capital elevated to a supreme social principle. Marx and his partner Engels envisaged the possibility of workers taking advantage of their concentration in industrial cities to win control of machine production for the common good. This idea that people might put machines and money to the ends of economic democracy is still with us in the age of digital technologies and it is no nearer being realized than a century and a half ago. The main difference is that machines and society were becomingly strongly centralized then and may be subject to the opposite tendency now.

At the beginning of the twentieth century, Georg Simmel asked how human personality and personal relations were being transformed by the increasingly impersonal society of large cities. In his essay, "The metropolis and mental life," he focused on how people were drawn together physically in these huge agglomerations and bombarded by multitudinous signs and sensations at high speed. As a result they retreated into paying less attention to the individual qualities of others and into seeking a personal autonomy that was to some extent guaranteed by the anonymity of the crowd. If classical liberalism sought individual freedom of movement as a way of escaping the social restrictions of the old regime, this new individualism was based more on the desire to distinguish oneself from others as a unique personality within a mass culture whose size and objective spirit were palpable. In small-scale pre-industrial societies, production and consumption were linked by exchanges between people who usually knew each other and money was a marginal factor. Now mass production and consumption were linked in world markets where most parties were unknown to each other and money pervaded the economic process. The social psychology of metropolitans was thus dominated by detachment and by indifference to the qualities of people and things. Intellectual culture and money economy reproduced these attitudes separately and together, in that both privilege abstract simplification and rational calculation, while neglecting those features of individuality that cannot be reduced to logic and numbers.

Simmel's analysis points to a general transformation of individual personality by the experience of living in mass society. This internalization of impersonal norms makes it hard for us to break out of the restrictions they impose on us. The question is whether the digital revolution in global communications has altered the balance of social life in a more hopeful direction. But, before turning to that issue, we need first to investigate more closely the relationship between markets, private property and rise of the modern corporation.

Private property: a short history

We experience the economy in modern society as a network of exchange relations. Most often these exchanges take place through the medium of money: the buyer hands over money to the seller in return for commodities. The sum total of these transactions is sometimes referred to as "the market," an abstract entity whose extent is unknowable. It is only in recent decades that people everywhere have become linked up in a single nexus of exchange, "the world market." It is part of the ideology of modern markets that they can take place any time, anywhere and that the individuals involved are independent of and unknown to each other. This assumption ("economic individualism") enables economists to construct mathematical models of great generality, since they are conceived of initially as referring to behavior outside time, place and society. The institutional conditions that make this assumption plausible are quite abnormal and were won at first in a few countries only after centuries of political struggle. The idea of buyers and sellers being free to make decisions concerning the price and volume of commodities to be transferred between them is pretty remarkable, even when all that is at stake is an artifact like a pair of shoes or a hat; but imagine the complications when the commodity being traded is someone's ability to work or a place for a family to live in.

The idea of personal agency in market situations is closely tied to that of private property. Private property is the ability of an individual owner to command exclusive rights over something against the rest of the world. We assume that, once we have bought an item, we can do what we like with it; the seller in turn has even greater freedom to dispose of the money we paid for it. Take a look at your personal possessions. They are yours. How did you get them and what gives you the right to think of them as your own? Your watch, for example, is clearly your own private property. It feels as if it is yours simply by virtue of being worn next to your skin. You probably bought it or it was a gift from someone who bought it. Market exchange is therefore the source of your right to claim the watch. But what secures the market exchange? Most people barely think about this, until something goes wrong. You get mugged on a dark night and the stranger demands your watch. In your fear and anger you now realize that the government underwrites your claim to own the watch and promises to restrict violent assaults on persons and property. Perhaps you resent the inadequate level of policing for a time; but eventually you settle back into thinking of your possessions as your own and forget about the social conditions that make it possible.

This idea of private property being secured by an anonymous state apparatus has been very rare in human history. More typically it was understood that ownership is relative to membership of concrete social groups capable of stopping others from infringing the right to control what belongs to us. In the extreme case, exchange is carried out by clans or similar groups acting as undifferentiated units. More usually individual claims to ownership are modified by such groups asserting a collective over-right, in contrast with the presumptively absolute individual ownership characteristic of private property. Take the following fictitious example as a case in point.

A Maasai warrior works as a night-watchman in Kenya's capital, Nairobi. The Maasai are famous for having maintained a traditional way of life based on cattle-herding and young men are formed into groups of warriors whose task is to defend the herds against all-comers. Nowadays many of them work temporarily for wages, often in jobs which require a watered down version of their warrior training. This migrant saves money and, before returning home, buys some commodities, including a watch which he wears on his wrist. On arriving back at his village, he meets an age-mate who says, "I like your watch: give it to me" and he must give it up. Why? Because all property in the village is held by virtue of the ability of warriors to ward off predators, both animal and human; and their solidarity, essential in battle, is undermined by any tendency of individuals to differentiate their own interests from those of the rest. They assert that a man's wife belongs to all his age-mates, even though it would be rare for sexual access to be demanded by one of them as a right. Our ex-watchman must be taught to recognize that life in the village still rests on different principles from those obtaining in Nairobi, and he hands over the watch.

In western legal history the Romans are credited with having invented private property. Before they achieved a strong state linked to extensive markets, property rights were based on the same ability of local kin-groups to assert their interests against similar groups. This was called *ius in personam* and it stated that rights over things are always mediated by concrete personal ties. In societies such as this ownership was derived from either production or consumption: something belonged to you because you had made it or because you needed to use it; and both kinds of right were exercised through membership of local groups. Traders on the other hand wanted to hold property in a wholly different sense: they needed to secure the right to own something they had neither produced themselves nor would use personally, but rather intended to sell for money. Moreover, they were exposed to the brigandage of any small group wishing to enforce its own local monopoly of violence. In the interest of furthering long-distance trade, the

Roman state offered military protection to these private merchants. It supported their claim to *ius in rem*, rights over things unmediated by personal relationships, in other words, the same system of private property that we now take so much for granted.

So, in order to allow the free circulation of commodities in exchange for money, both the connection between persons and objects and that between persons in groups were weakened in law. Yet physical association between persons and objects is still quite strong for modern English-speakers ("possession is nine-tenths of the law"), even if the social ties that make ownership possible have receded to the point of invisibility in the face of an atomizing economic ideology. This bears on the historical relationship between markets and the political project of liberal democracy.

In 1683, at the age of 51, John Locke was an unpublished Oxford academic and the client of a discredited politician. During the exclusion crisis of the Catholic King James II's accession to the throne, he fled for his life to Holland and was sacked by his college. He returned to England six years later after William of Orange's establishment of a Protestant monarchy in the Glorious Revolution of 1688. He immediately published *Two Treatises of Government*. Locke was subsequently appointed to the Board of Trade and wrote influential pamphlets on money that helped to resolve the recoinage crisis of the 1690s. Long before his death in 1704 he had become so famous that one of his correspondents could describe him without irony as "the greatest man in the world." As an architect of the middle-class revolution, Locke was certainly the leading public intellectual in the period when the United Kingdom was formed, along with the Bank of England, the national debt and some other durable economic institutions. The eighteenth century Enlightenment was largely a European response to his work. The Americans wrote their constitution (fruit of the first anti-colonial revolution) on the basis of his ideas. Now he is often regarded as an apologist for capitalism and the main source for a narrow "possessive individualism" on which neo-classical economics is founded.

When I finally got round to reading Locke's *Two Treatises of Government*, I did not find in them the story of economic individualism I had been led to expect. The purpose of his Commonwealth was to preserve everyone's property in themselves and their possessions. "The end of law is... to preserve and enlarge freedom." Freedom is "...a liberty to dispose and order, as he lists, his person, actions, possessions and his whole property within the allowance of those laws under which he is, and therein not to be subject to the arbitrary will of another, but freely follow his own." The main emphasis is on the political conditions of personal autonomy. Both treatises turn out to be extended essays on the theme of parent-child relations. In the first, Locke denies the right of absolute monarchs to claim to be the father of their subjects. In the second, he allows only one exception to the rule of autonomy of citizens and that is childhood. He asks how we can protect children so that they grow up to be independent. This is a contradiction that no society has yet solved and it explains why he was best-known in eighteenth-century England for *Some Thoughts Concerning Education*, a treatise notable for his advocacy of potty training, rather than for his political theories or epistemology.

Locke also asked how one Commonwealth acting alone can protect the property of foreigners passing through it—Who or what secures the property of the Dutchman in London?—opening up the issue of cosmopolitan society beyond the boundaries of states that Kant addressed more squarely a century later. Yet he should be seen as the founder of national capitalism, long before Hegel and Bismarck. His main aim was to establish the infrastructure of global trade for the following century with Britain at its centre. Above all, he wanted to stabilize the means of communication and exchange—words and money. For him, there were economic criminals and semantic criminals. The state can hang counterfeiters, but what do you do with politicians who never say what they mean? Each undermines confidence in civil society. Only a perverse hindsight, warped by what capitalism later became, would represent this urgent and far-sighted political project as a way of masking class dominance through a rhetoric of market democracy and natural rights.

The classical liberal revolutions of the seventeenth to mid-nineteenth centuries (the English Civil War, the Glorious Revolution, the American War of Independence, the French Revolution, Britain's Anti-Corn Law movement and Italy's Risorgimento) were aimed at transferring power from the traditional rulers, the military aristocracy and landlord class, to the owners of money capital who claimed to represent the interests of all the rest. In particular they sought to secure property in their own commercial gains that had hitherto been subject to predation by specialists in violence close to the king. The next step was to discipline workers to accept the impersonal regime of factory production. But, with a few state-licensed exceptions like the East India Company and the Bank of England, capitalist businesses were owned and run by individual entrepreneurs who were personally exposed to the erratic swings of markets. The addition of machines to production on a large scale drew millions of workers into burgeoning cities. There they started agitating for a better deal in the factories and society at large. At the same time criminal gangs took over large swathes of the urban economy. This set the stage for the linked political revolutions of the 1860s ushering in a new phase of industrial capitalism dominated by nation-states and business corporations. These included the American civil war, the abolition of serfdom in Russia, the culmination of Italy's Risorgimento, Britain's democratic reforms and the formation of the Anglo-Indian super-state, Japan's Meiji restoration, the unification of Germany and, following defeat in the Franco-Prussian war, the French third republic. In the same decade, Marx published *Capital*. The globalization of the "national capitalism" born at this time is the immediate context for our current political and intellectual problems.

In order to understand the possibilities entailed in our moment of history, we need to grasp what has happened to private property in the last century and a half. Huge social entities, especially national governments and corporations operating on a transnational scale, have acquired what were once the property rights of individual citizens in order to manage the agglomerations of machines and money that dominate our world. Far from shoring up liberal democracy, private property in this guise favors its totalitarian alternative, where personal identity is made to conform to the needs of impersonal institutions. It will pay us to visit briefly the origins of this process.

If a sole proprietorship or partnership owes more money than its assets are worth, the original investors are personally responsible for the debt. In 1580, Queen Elizabeth I of England granted "limited freedom from liability" to The Golden Hind, a ship owned by Sir Francis Drake in which she was the largest shareholder. This meant that, if the enterprise incurred large debts, investors were limited in their liability only to the amount of their initial investment, leaving creditors to pick up the rest of the losses. In fact, the returns on this low-risk investment were 5,000 percent and the Queen was well-pleased. Drake became a national hero, but the rest of the world thought of him as a pirate. The business model they invented underlies the modern corporation. At the time, world trade was dominated by the Dutch; so Queen Elizabeth granted a charter in 1600 to the East India Company, a group of merchants and aristocrats based on the City of London. Over the next two centuries this grew to a considerable size without ever losing its close ties to national government.

Elihu Yale was the company's governor in Madras before endowing the college that gratefully changed its name to his. Apart from its well-known role in India, the East India Company financed James Cook's explorations of the Pacific and controlled international trade with the American colonies. The price of expansion in competition with the Dutch was high, however, and by the 1770s the company was on the verge of bankruptcy. Dutch traders and American smugglers (whom the company wanted to be prosecuted as "pirates") were by-passing the company's monopoly to sell cheaper tea to the small businesses supplying the lucrative American market. The Tea Act of 1773 gave the East India Company the exclusive right to sell tea to the American colonies, exempted it from taxes levied on exports to America and granted a tax refund on 17 million pounds of tea then stored unsold in England. This substantially increased the company's profitability (the King was a major stockholder) and allowed it to undercut the prices charged by the many small businesses retailing tea in America. The Boston tea party was fuelled by resentment at being made the victims of corporate monopoly in this way.

Thomas Jefferson saw three main threats to democracy—governing elites, organized religion and commercial monopolists (whom he referred to as "pseudo-aristocrats"). With the above precedent in mind, it is hardly surprising that he was keen to include freedom from monopoly in the Bill of Rights. But, mainly thanks to his Federalist opponents, that particular clause slipped through the cracks of the constitution. From then on it was a consistent goal of corporations to win the constitutional rights of individual citizens for their businesses. This aim was largely thwarted, but it built up momentum in the aftermath of the Civil War, when the railroads acquired wealth and power that they were anxious to convert into legal privilege. The Fourteenth Amendment of 1868 sought to guarantee former slaves the equal protection of the laws, by making illegal discriminatory provision of education, for example. This provision was then used by the railroads to sue states and local authorities for regulations enacted specifically to control them, on the grounds that this created "different classes of persons." The issue of corporate personhood was widely debated in the newspapers of the day. With their wealth and longevity, the corporations could keep coming back to the courts until they won. And eventually they did, through the Supreme Court judgment of 1886 in the case of *Santa Clara County vs. the Southern Pacific Railroad*.

The railroad was being sued by the county for back taxes, but its lawyers claimed that the company was a person entitled to human rights under the Fourteenth Amendment. The written record of the Supreme Court's judgment says:

> The defendant corporations are persons within the intent of the clause in section of the Fourteenth Amendment of the Constitution of the United States, which forbids a State to deny to any person within its jurisdiction the equal protection of the laws.

Thom Hartmann, whose book *Unequal Protection* is a major source for this part of my essay, believes that it was not Chief Justice Waite's intention to draw this conclusion, which was rather inserted into the head notes for the case (which do not constitute legal precedent) by J.C. Bancroft Davis, the Supreme Court's reporter. Davis was not a low-level hack: a Harvard-educated lawyer, he had been a judge, Assistant Secretary of State and Minister to the German Empire (in which capacity he met Karl Marx). He wrote a dozen books, was once president of a railroad company and worked with railroad barons such as Jay Cooke in the 1860s. Whatever its provenance, this judgment opened the floodgates: in the following quarter-century, of over 300 Fourteenth Amendment cases considered by the Supreme Court, almost all were brought by corporations claiming the rights of natural persons; only nineteen involved African Americans.

Today, if a town in upper New York state wants to protect its small shopkeepers by denying Walmart the right to open a superstore there, it will risk facing an expensive lawsuit brought to defend the corporation's constitutional rights as a person. It may be worth recalling William Jennings Bryan's observation that corporations and living people, artificial and real persons,

> differ in the purpose for which they were created, in the strength which they possess and in the restraints under which they act. Man is the handiwork of God and was placed upon earth to carry

out a Divine purpose; the corporation is the handi-
work of man and created to carry out a money-
making policy. There is comparatively little difference in the strength of men; a corporation may be
one hundred, one thousand or even one million
times stronger than the average man. Man acts
under the restraints of conscience, and is influenced
also by a belief in a future life. A corporation has
no soul and cares nothing about the hereafter…

Today God's purpose is routinely invoked to
justify a US government beholden to the corporations
in a way that would surprise even the East India
Company's shareholders whose excesses did so much
to provoke the war of independence.

We still think of private property as belonging
to living persons and oppose private and public
spheres on that basis. But what makes property private
is holding exclusive rights against the world. Abstract
entities like governments and corporations, as well as
individuals, can thus hold private property. We are
understandably confused by this development, especially since the rise to public power of the corporations rested substantially on collapsing the difference
between real and artificial persons in economic law.
But of course corporations have retained that limited
liability for bad debts and freedom from some other
legal hindrances that you and I still suffer from. This
constitutes a major obstacle not only to the practice of
democracy, but also to thinking about it. We find it
hard enough as it is to see ourselves as equal and free
agents in a democracy where power is exercised
remotely ands anonymously. But if we swallow the

idea that General Motors deserves the same protection of the laws as individual citizens, then we are lost. And the sad truth is that many intellectuals have followed the same path in obscuring the distinction between living persons and abstractions, as well as that between people, things and ideas.

Private property has not only evolved from individual ownership to predominately corporate forms, but its main point of reference has also shifted from "real" to "intellectual" property, that is from material objects to ideas. This is partly because of the digital revolution in communications that has led to the economic preponderance of information services whose reproduction and transmission is often costless or nearly so. How copyright, patents and trademarks came to assume such significance in the transnational corporate economy will be the subject of a later section. Here it is enough to point out that a similar sleight of hand is at work as in the claim to corporate personhood. If I steal your cow, its loss is material, since only one of us can benefit from its milk. But if I copy a CD or DVD, I am denying no-one access to it.

Yet corporate lobbyists depend precisely on this misleading analogy to influence courts and legislators to treat duplication of their "property" as "theft" or even "piracy." It is ironic that the United States, born in an act of resistance against corporate monopoly, should now be foisting onto smaller countries an intellectual property treaty that shores up the monopoly profits of transnational corporations on pain of denying those countries access to the American market.

The Digital Revolution

To repeat, what matters in this world is money,
machines and people, in that order. Our political task
is to reverse the order. But most intellectuals know
very little about any of them, being preoccupied with
their own production of ideas. The social scientists are
particularly culpable, with their addiction to impersonal abstractions and suppression of individual
subjectivity. But even the humanists seem to have
abandoned people in their pursuit of theoretical ideas.
We need a new humanism appropriate to a world
dominated by the impersonal power of money and
machines. The hit man's dilemma comes from experi-
encing the world as a conflict between his inner
subjectivity and the objective conditions of his social

role. His sense of himself as a good person inside contrasts with what he does outside. Fiction (novels, movies, plays) normally does a better job of capturing this tension than the writings of professional thinkers. Moreover, the audience enters the plot imaginatively in a way that allows for the free interplay of subjectivity and history in microcosm. We want to integrate the inside and the outside, the personal and the impersonal, but the idea of a moral politics combining them often seems unattainable.

Each of us embarks on a journey outward into the world and inward into the self. We are, as Durkheim said, at once collective and individual. Society is mysterious to us because we have lived in it and it now dwells inside us at a level that is not ordinarily visible from the perspective of everyday life. Writing and reading fiction bring the two into a relationship that we can share with others. Travel also exposes us to society in different forms. So one method for understanding world society would be to make an ongoing practice of trying to synthesize these varied experiences, to make a world as singular as the self. There are as many worlds as individuals and their journeys; and, even if there were only one out there, each of us changes it whenever we make a move. Our task is to scale the world down and the self up so that they can enter into a meaningful relationship. Again stories allow the two to meet on more equal terms than in real life. Telling stories and listening to them involve communication, a process whereby we express what is in our minds and hope that others can somehow receive the message in theirs. This section asks how human communication is evolving in the context of the latest phase of the machine revolution and whether that favors the integration we seek or the opposite.

Communication is a word cognate with common and community. It appears to have its root in the ability of a group or network of people to exchange things and ideas through interaction. This usually takes the form either of the circulation of material objects by means of money or the exchange of signs by means of language. The two circuits are converging in the digital revolution of our day: money is becoming information and information money. In both cases, the signs exchanged are now increasingly virtual, meaning that they take the form of bits detached from persons and places passing through the ether at the speed of light. This process of digitization defines our moment in history; but the precedents for it go back to the origin of writing and beyond.

Information is an intentional signal from the perspective of the sender, perhaps anything that reduces the uncertainty of a receiver. The transmission of information through machines has traditionally come in the form of waves, imperceptible gradations of light and sound. For communications engineers, analog and digital computation rest on measuring and counting, respectively: on the one hand, continuous changes in physical variables like age, height, warmth or speed; on the other, discontinuous leaps between discrete entities, such as days of the week, dollars and cents, letters of the alphabet, named individuals. Analog processes, such as time and distance, can be represented digitally; but it was something of a breakthrough for early modern science to measure continuous physical change with precision. Before that the clarity of phenomena was generally enhanced and comparison facilitated by constructing bounded entities that could be counted, by digitization.

Digital numeration is at its clearest when the only possible signals are binary: on/off, yes/no, either/or, 0/1. And this reversion to an older system of simple enumeration lies behind the latest revolution in communications. Digitization greatly increases the speed and reliability of information processing and transmission; it also lies behind the rapid convergence of what were once discrete systems—telephones, television, computers—in a worldwide network of communications, the internet. Computers have been digital from the beginning, while the other two have almost completed the shift from sound waves to digital transmission. As a result, any kind of information can be carried by all types of equipment, which become essentially substitutable. Communications technology in future will consist in various combinations of screen, computer and transmitter/receiver. The manufacturing monopolists will fight over whether the resulting hybrids resemble more a television set, a PC or a telephone. But the process common to all is digitization and the present moment of convergence lends our era its specificity. In order to place the internet within a broader context of social life, we should step back to examine its historical antecedents.

Human communication starts out as speech and the words exchanged are usually between people who can see as well as hear each other. A lot of non-verbal information accompanies the words—gestures, tone, emanations of feeling—and this helps us to interpret what is said and how to respond. The words are abstract enough; but the exchange is face-to-face, grounding what passes between us in the exigency of place. Writing made it possible to detach meaning from the persons and places where it was generated and to communicate at some distance in time and space. Even then, the signs were often highly particular, too many for all but a select few to understand and variable from one scribe to the next. The alphabet took the process of simplifying the signs a step further, one sound for one unambiguous letter, thereby making it possible for writing to be adopted more widely and reliably. It was, if you will, a cheapening of the cost of transmitting information.

The Phoenician city states, maritime traders of the Lebanese coast, were the main pioneers of alphabetic writing at the beginning of the first millennium BC; and it came into Europe through the Greeks. I like to speculate how books were received at first. For example on Homer:

> All youngsters want to do today is read at home.
> You can't get them to go out or anything. They
> have no idea what it was like hearing the old boy in
> a torch-lit barn on a Saturday night, with his voice
> echoing in the rafters. It brought tears to your eyes.
> Well, some of it was the smoke too.

Many more people have since had access to the bard than could ever have been in the same room as him during his lifetime, even if reading is less sensational than witnessing a live performance. Virtual communication takes place more in the mind than in actual fact. The only way people could escape from the restrictions of the here and now was through exercising their imagination, usually under the stimulus of story-telling. Alphabetic writing, ultimately the book, vastly increased the scope of the collective imagination. It also made easier the conduct of business at distance.

At the same time as the alphabet (around 700 BC), coinage was invented in Lydia, now a part of Turkey. Alphabetic writing and this new form of money were profoundly subversive of old ways. Until then, wealth and power were concrete and visible, being attached to the people who had them. They took the form of cattle, vineyards, buildings, armed men and beautiful women. Now riches could be concealed as gold coins, allowing for a double detachment from persons—impersonal exchange at distance and unaccountable economic power (because hidden and private). From the beginning, writing found a ready application in palace bureaucracy. The king could send messages while remaining himself invisible. It is one thing to be beaten up by royal thugs; but imagine the terror of receiving a written message saying "please commit suicide before tomorrow." We feel something of this dread whenever we receive a tax demand from the unseen hand of a remote authority.

Plato captures this in a story he tells in *The Republic*. Gyges was one of the Lydian king's servants. The king had a ring that made him invisible. He took Gyges with him one night to spy on his wife getting ready for bed. Gyges and the wife eventually ganged up to kill the king. Gyges got the ring, the wife and the kingdom, making him a precursor of legendary rich rulers like Midas. This myth expresses the contradictions widely felt at the time between visible, personal society and invisible, impersonal society. The Greeks were very concerned about the security of contracts between strangers. They insisted that each contract (for which they devised the word symbolon) should be marked by an object like a ring split in the presence of both parties and a witness. They didn't quite believe in pieces of paper.

As long as books were hand-written, their circulation was restricted to a small literate elite capable of copying and reading them. In my old university, Cambridge, until the sixteenth century, teachers carried their own scrolls around in the deep pockets of their gowns and read them out for payment to students who thereby ended up with their own copies. Copying was not in itself a major obstacle to the diffusion of texts. The ability to interpret the texts was scarce and costly. Printing made it possible for many more people to get hold of written material; and it eliminated some of the ambiguities of handwriting. It took a line of business away from the hacks with gowns and shifted the emphasis in learning to the act of interpretation and hence to understanding. When my students complained of a "lack of structure" in my lectures, meaning that they wanted to be told the half dozen points that, when memorized by rote, would ensure a decent pass in the exams, I would ask them to consider the success of Cambridge University Press over the last 450 years. This was built on putting books directly into the hands of students, so that they could make up their own minds what they meant, with the help of learned and hopefully inspiring teachers. Instead, today's students wanted me to revert to the role of a reader of scrolls before the print revolution, passing signs from one person to the next without engaging the minds of either.

My grandmother was born before the car, radio, telephone, the movies, air travel and all the other transport and communications technologies that came to dominate twentieth-century society. I used to marvel at the way she adapted to all of them. Now I am beginning to understand what she had to put up with. For, having started out in the Second World War, I realize how profoundly my world has changed in these respects. I grew up without television in the home and with very limited opportunities for travel; so I relied on books to get away from it all. It feels as if my intensive training in the manipulation of words and numbers now belongs to another age. I have managed to gain a toehold in the digital revolution, largely with the tolerant assistance of bright young people who have grown up with it. For them, the phase of national television that I missed is already a bygone era. We all enter this extraordinary time with a bundle of advantages and drawbacks. I take pride in a facility for writing coherent e-mail messages at a pace somewhere between a letter and a phone-call. Yet I also know that communicating through keyboards will soon be replaced by audio-visual methods, thereby removing one more link between the book and the screen. My academic colleagues are still fighting the war against television, refusing to allow one into a living room designed to show off their books. It's all relative.

Face-to-face exchanges, instead of being displaced by telecommunications, take on an added value when one spends the working day in front of a computer screen. Simple pursuits like reading and conversation, which used to be taken for granted when they monopolized our means of communication, can be approached in a more analytical and creative frame of mind, now that there are so many other ways of acquiring and transmitting ideas. I do most of my writing in a Paris apartment, the long-distance writer's traditional retreat into privacy; nothing new there. But I also keep up e-mail exchanges with friends living all over the world. And no writer was able to do that before the 1990s. I now have a virtual office to accommodate a life of movement, my laptop; but I was forced to recognize the value of my own memory when it was stolen. Each of us experiences the digital revolution in our own way; yet there are changes taking place that affect us all.

Computers have been with us for over 50 years, television for a bit longer and telephones for twice that long, but their convergence in the internet is little more than a decade old. All messages are transmitted between computers and television screens (hardware) by means of telephone and radio signals. The infrastructure for these transmissions in turn constitutes a rapidly evolving network of satellites, cable grids and other means. The internet is the most inclusive term for all the electronic networks in the world. It is the network of networks. These are decentralized to a large extent, but they constitute a conceptual unity in much the same way as "the world market" does. Indeed the latter's transactions increasingly take place on the internet. The World Wide Web is a disembodied machine, a type of software whose protocols were published in 1991 for use on the internet. The big innovation then was the move from words and numbers to visual images; and at first it was used to display messages in a non-interactive multimedia format; but its potential for more interactive participation is becoming more obvious now.

The internet was for several decades restricted in use to a strategic complex of military, academic and business interests, based in the United States and Europe. For some time, its most intensive use was between physicists located near the two main nuclear accelerators in Illinois and Geneva. These scientists lent to the medium its definitive style and content in the early decades: highly technical, closed and clubby. By the time that the internet went public in 1993, there were only three million users in the world. In the next five years the number of users increased to 100 million. This figure is estimated in 2005 to be over 800 million or 1 in 8 people alive. In the last five years the number of internet users tripled in Africa, Latin America and the Middle East and doubled in

North America and Europe, with Asia between the two. No previous technology has diffused so fast through the world's population. If ever there was a challenge to empiricism, the habit of extrapolating from previous experience, it is trying to guess what the social impact of all this is likely to be.

Compare, for example, the adoption of iron in the lands bordering the Eastern Mediterranean 3,000 years ago. Iron is the commonest metal ore on earth and it is extremely robust and malleable. When the technique of smelting it was first discovered, small quantities of iron were used principally for prestigious ornaments worn by the ruling class. Then it found a military use as weapons that allowed some groups to gain a temporary advantage over their neighbors. It took several hundred years in most cases for iron to find its most significant application, as tools used in the production of food and manufactures by the common people. If you had happened to be living in Assyria, say, at the beginning of iron production, you would have guessed that its destiny was to be a symbolic and practical means of maintaining the dominance of a military caste. Much the same inference could have been drawn in relation to the internet at any time during the Cold War.

So what is the digital revolution? It consists of rapid changes in the size, cost and especially speed of machines capable of processing information. This is now measured as millions of instructions per second or MIPS. The world's first computer, the Electronic Numerical Integrator and Computer (ENIAC), was built soon after the Second World War. It cost millions of dollars, was 50 meters wide and 3 meters tall, and processed 5,000 instructions per second. Twenty-five years later, an Intel micro-processor chip, 12 mm square, cost $200 and processed 60,000 instructions per second (0.06 MIPS). Today Pentium 4 chips have a processing capacity of 10,000 MIPS and this is expected to reach 100,000 MIPS by 2012. In 1980 copper phone wires transmitted information at the rate of a page of print a second; today, hair-thin optical fibers can transmit the equivalent of almost a million encyclopedia volumes per second. Until recently the modems (linking computers and tele-phones) most commonly in use took an hour to down-load a five-minute video. Broadband technology can now perform the same operation in ten seconds. Already the Americans are building the next stage, "Internet2," like the first internet a collaboration between universities, government and industry, where a full-length movie can be downloaded in three minutes.

The table that follows puts this contemporary cascade of technical change in context. There are three main stages of the machine revolution, marked by steam-power, electricity grids and information-processing, respectively. The steam-engine was invented in 1712; but it was another sixty years before James Watt's improvements made it feasible to power factories by this means; and the industrial revolution proper did not take off until the 1820s. Electricity was first identified and harnessed in 1831; over fifty years later, Thomas Edison began generating it for public use. Again, only in the early twentieth century was the

efficiency of factories transformed by the wholesale
adoption of electric motors; and widespread domestic
use of electrical appliances had to wait until the 1950s.
It took a hundred years from Faraday's discovery until
80% of Americans were supplied with electricity at
home.

Three Stages of the Machine Revolution

	c.1800	c.1900	c.2000
Revolution	Industrial	Bureaucratic	Digital
Technology	Steam-power	Electricity grids	Information processors
Social form	Factory	Office	Internet
Business	Individual entrepreneurs	State/corporate partnership	Transnational corporations
Market	Urban	National	World

If ENIAC is analogous to the inventions of
Newcomen and Faraday, our time bears comparison
with those moments, half a century later, when the
discovery first began to have widespread social application. It will be decades before we can tell how society is
being affected. Steam-power allowed factories to be
located away from their principal source of energy
(once water and wood, then coal) and to deploy
machines replacing manual labour. These factories

were operated by a new class of industrial entrepreneurs, individuals like Richard Arkwright who were later parodied in Dickens' novels. Electricity helped turn factory production into a streamlined system of managerial control, powered the office complexes of the bureaucratic revolution and eventually made domestic life more convenient. It required a physical network for its distribution and this encouraged governments to own or licence monopoly operators of grids as the most tangible symbols of national capitalism.

The internet permits almost instantaneous communication between machines using microscopic circuits to process and store information. There are profound implications for the system of money. Now that the internet is no longer primarily a research tool, its use is increasingly as an electronic marketplace, making links between and within businesses and between them and their customers. Electricity travels at the speed of light and the transfer of information itself is essentially costless. This then is a market with unusual time and space dimensions, where the personal and impersonal aspects of economic life meet on new terms. Very little of social significance will be left untouched before long.

The world economy is being transformed once more by radical reductions in the cost of producing a basic commodity, in this case the transfer of information. There was a time when commodities traded internationally were things extracted from the ground and services were performed locally in person. Now the person answering your business call could be located anywhere in the world and a growing number of service jobs are exposed to global competition. Vast profits are to be made in entertainment, education, the media, finance, software and all the other information services. But the digital revolution poses specific problems for accumulation. The saying goes that "information wants to be free" and certainly there is continuous downward pressure on prices in this sector arising from the ease of copying proprietary products. We will examine this issue at greater length in the next section. But there is another aspect of this revolution that bears directly on the relationship between the personal and impersonal dimensions of social life.

The cheapening of the cost of information transfers has considerable consequence for the character of long-distance market relations. Money was traditionally impersonal so that it could retain its value when it moved between people who might not even know each other. If you drop a coin or banknote on the floor, whoever picks it up can spend it just as easily as you can. Money in this form is an instrument detached from the persons who use it. The expansion of trade often depended on this objectivity of the medium of exchange and economists have long debated whether money's value derives from its being a scarce commodity or from the guarantees made by states who issued it. Bank credit on the other hand has always been more directly personal, being linked to the trustworthiness of individuals and, in the case of paper instruments such as checks, issued by them. The idea that transactions involving money are essentially amoral comes from its impersonal form, but until recently, in most societies, the bulk of economic life was carried out by people who knew each other and were able to discriminate between individuals on the basis of experience.

The transition to impersonal economic institutions came suddenly. The novelist Arnold Bennett describes for the English Potteries the appearance of the phenomenon of fixed posted prices. People were used to engaging with shopkeepers personally; and each purchase took place under particular circumstances, involving variable price, quality and credit terms, all of them based on the specific relationship between trader and customer. Bennett recalls the shock of encountering for the first time goods identified by little white cards with non-negotiable prices on them. That was little more than a century ago, yet most western consumers today find sliding prices to be almost as threatening as beggars in the street. The bureaucratic revolution in the decades around 1900 saw the first department stores, concentrating under one roof a wide range of commodities which would previously have been sold in separate shops. This is where fixed prices came from. The shift towards more impersonal forms of economic organization had important consequences for marketing. Bureaucracies limit the personal discretion of employees, hedging their activities around with rules that can only be broken at risk of dismissal. In the new stores, customers dealt face-to-face with assistants who had no power to negotiate. That power rested with owners and managers who were now removed from the point of sale, unlike the small shopkeeper. The main imperative of management was to control subordinates; and this ethos stretched back to the production lines as well as outwards to an anonymous market of consumers whose tastes were manipulated by public advertising.

The era of mass production and consumption may be ending as a result of cheap information transfers. It is now possible to attach a lot of information about individuals to transactions at distance. For example, amazon.com keeps a record of every book I have bought from them and they make recommendations for new purchases on this basis. This is similar to the small bookseller who reserves a book for a favorite customer, but it all takes place anonymously at distance. Some firms are already moving towards a system known as Customer Retail Maintenance (CRM) based on data banks that know no limit in scope. This enables them to target buyers who generate above average revenues, to remind them of the need to buy something for their wife's birthday and so on. Nowhere has this process gone further than in the market for personal credit. A generation ago I relied on the bank manager to extend my purchasing power through making an overdraft available. Now the number and variety of financial instruments on offer is growing exponentially and these are often customized to my personal needs. It is not quite the same as ordering a suit from Savile Row in the nineteenth century, but the trend is definitely to restore personal identity to what were until not long ago largely impersonal contracts. Of course, rich and powerful organizations have access to huge processors with which to manipulate an often unknowing public. But at the very least, for many people, these developments have introduced new conditions of engagement with the impersonal economy. What matters is to recognize that the line between personal and impersonal society is shifting, with significant implications for individual and collective agency.

The digital revolution is driven by a desire to replicate at distance or by means of computers experiences that we normally associate with face-to-face human encounters. All communication, whether the exchange of words or money, has a virtual aspect in that symbols and their media of circulation stand for what people really do for each other. It usually involves the exercise of imagination, an ability to construct meanings across the gap between symbol and reality. The power of the book depended on sustaining that leap of faith. In that sense, capitalism was always virtual. Indeed Marx tried to show how the power of money was mystified through its appearance as things (coins, products, machinery) rather than as relations between living people. Both Marx and Weber insisted that capitalists sought to detach their money-making activities, as far as possible, from real conditions obstructing their purposes. Money-lending, the practice of charging interest on loans without any intervening act of production or exchange, is one of the oldest forms of capitalism. So the idea of the money circuit becoming separated from reality is hardly new.

The point of the virtual is abstraction and this is a function of the shift to ever more inclusive levels of exchange, to the world market as the frame for economic activity rather than the nation-state. But more abstract forms of communication allow real persons to be involved with each other at distance in very concrete ways. The idea of "virtual reality" expresses this double movement: on the one hand machines whose complexity their users cannot possibly understand, on the other live experiences "as good as" real. It is the same with money. Capitalism has become virtual in two main senses: the shift from material production (agriculture and manufacturing) to information services; and the corresponding detachment of the circulation of money from production and trade. Since the invention of money futures in 1975, the world market for financial instruments has mushroomed to the point where less than 1% of the money traded internationally is used to buy goods and services; the rest is just money in one form being exchanged for money in another. And this money market, sometimes referred to just as "the markets," is largely unregulated by political institutions.

If we would make a better world, rather than just contemplate it, we must learn to think creatively in terms that reflect reality and reach out for imagined possibilities. This in turn depends on capturing what is essential about the world we live in, its movement and direction, not just its stable forms. The idea of "virtual reality" expresses the form of movement common to both narrative and dialectic—extension from the actual to the possible. "Virtual" means existing in the mind, but not in fact. When combined with "reality," it means a product of the imagination that is almost but not quite real. In technical terms, "virtual reality" is a computer simulation that enables the effects of operations to be shown in real time. The word "real" connotes something genuine, authentic, serious. In philosophy it means existing objectively in the world; in economics actual purchasing power; in law fixed, landed property; in optics an image formed by the convergence of light rays in space; and in mathematics, real numbers are, of course, not imaginary. "Reality" is present, in time and space; and its opposite is imagined connection at distance, something as old as story-telling and books, but now given a new impetus by the internet. The experience of near synchrony at distance, the compression of time and space, is already altering our conceptions of social relationships, of place and movement.

The digital divide between people with and without access to the internet, the "wired" elite versus the "unwired" masses, is a pressing issue; but what concerns me here is how what we do offline influences what we do on it and vice versa. People often talk about cyberspace as if it were a self-contained universe, but each of us brings to it a personal bundle of social experience that is unique. Martin Heidegger said that "world" is an abstract metaphysical category (all that relates to or affects the life of a person) and its dialectical counterpart is "solitude," the idea of the isolated individual. Every human subject makes a world of his or her own whose center is the self. The world opens up only to the extent that we recognize ourselves as finite, as individual, and this should lead us to "finitude," the concrete specifics of time and place in which we necessarily live. So "world" is relative both to an abstract version of subjectivity and, more important, to our particularity in the world (seen as position and movement in time and space).

The idea that each of us lives alone (solitude) in a world largely of our own making, as opposed to the relational universe we inhabit most of the time, seems to be more real when we go online. But both terms are imagined as well as being reciprocal; they are equally abstract and untenable as an object of knowledge. We approach them from a relative location in society where we actually live. Therefore the social forms of the internet cannot be studied independently of what people bring to it from elsewhere. The life of people off-line is an invisible presence when they are on it. It would be wrong, however, to deny any autonomy at all to "virtual reality." Would we dream of reducing literature to the circumstances of readers? And this too is Heidegger's point. "World" and "solitude" may be artificial abstractions, but they do affect how we behave in "finitude."

I have tried to indicate how the digital revolution has the potential to turn the world of the twentieth century upside down. Its social effects will not be known for a considerable while, but we should recognize already that the relationship of individuals to society, economy and culture is now subject to far-reaching changes for which the precedents are not obvious. My focus in this essay is on the evolution of private property in particular and in the next section we will see how digitized commerce has spawned a war for control of the value generated by sales of information-based commodities. The slogan of this war is "intellectual property rights" and it announces a new phase in the history of political economy.

Intellectual property

Political economy emerged in the early nineteenth century as a discipline concerned with how the value generated by an expanding market economy might best be distributed in the interest of economic growth. Smith, Ricardo and their followers identified three types of resources, each thought to be endowed with the power of increase: the environment (land), money (capital) and human creativity (labor). These in turn were represented by their respective owners: landlords, capitalists and workers. The distribution of specific sources of income—rent, profit and wages—contained the key to the laws of political economy. The main conflict was then between landlords and capitalists; and the policy was to ensure that the value of market sales was not diverted from the capital fund to high rents.

Political economy held that competitive markets lowered the margins available to middle men and forced capitalists to reduce their production costs through innovations aimed at improving efficiency. This was achieved through economies of scale, division of labor and ultimately the introduction of machines to factories. The productivity of labor was raised, allowing the resulting profits to be ploughed back into an expanded level of activity. Society's manpower was thereby freed up for more elaborate forms of commercial production. The only threat to this upward spiral was if landowners raised their rents to take advantage of these newly profitable industries, diverting value into wasteful consumption. Worse, whereas the capital fund was inherently limitless, land was definitely in limited supply. Economic expansion meant population growth, driving up food prices and squeezing the capital fund on the other side through wages. The solution was to expose Britain's landowners to competition with cheap overseas suppliers; and this made free trade the great political issue of the 1840s.

The basic division between classes possessing the environment, money and human creativity persists today. Indeed, writers as diverse as Locke and Marx had visions of history in which a state of nature or society based on the land gives way to an age of money (our own) whose contradictions should lead to a just society based on fair reward for human creativity. So how are these broad classes of interest manifested in the struggle for the value generated by electronic commerce? If the owners of money and labor were first allied against the landlords (industrial capitalism), the capitalists later turned to the traditional specialists in crowd control, the landlord class, to help them hold down burgeoning urban populations (both factory workers and criminal gangs) concentrated in the cities by machine industry. This fusion of bureaucratic capitalism and the nation-state dominated the twentieth-century world. So how are the classes aligned in the present phase of global or virtual capitalism?

The landlord class has by no means rolled over and died; but the internet offers a means of escape from land shortage, indeed from spatial constraints of all kinds. The territorial controls once exercised by the landed aristocracy have largely now passed to national governments. Territorial states seek to extract taxes from all money transactions taking place inside or across the boundaries of their jurisdiction and also derive significant rents from public property such as mineral wealth. This has been greatly facilitated by the advances in bureaucracy made over the last 150 years; but it becomes more difficult when the source of value shifts from car factories and downtown shopping centers to commodity exchange conducted at the speed of light across borders. This system of involuntary transfers (taxation and rents on physical assets) could once be justified in terms of economic security for all. But that principle has been under attack by neo-conservative liberals for over two decades now.

The capitalists have come a long way too. Having formed an alliance with the traditional rulers from the 1860s onwards, they absorbed and ultimately defeated the challenge posed by the workers. The recent revival of free market liberalism provides triumphal evidence of that victory. But the relationship of capital to the state has become increasingly moot. Money has always had an international dimension and the corporations that dominate world capitalism today are less obviously tied to their nations of origin than before. There are now some three dozen firms with an annual turnover of $30-50 billion, larger than the GDP of all but eight countries. Moreover, half of the world's 500 largest firms are American and a third European. So the world economy is controlled today by a few firms of western origin, but with dubious national loyalties.

Ever since their merger, capital and the nation-state have had a relationship of conflict and co-operation. The wave of anti-trust legislation that accompanied the rise of monopolists like John D. Rockefeller in the early twentieth century is matched today by the feebler efforts of governments to contain the economic power of Microsoft and a few companies like it. Corporations now rely at least as much on rents (income from property secured by law) as on profits from sales of commodities; and so the burden of accumulation has shifted from workers to consumers. Governments compete for a share of the value of commodities in the form of taxes. But sales, rents and taxes all depend on a system of legal coercion, on a realistic threat of punishment, to make people pay up. So far the corporations have not found a way of dispensing with the state as enforcer, but this reliance is called into question when markets are increasingly international in scope.

So where does that leave the rest of us? If Marx and Engels could identify the general interest with a growing body of factory workers tied to machines owned by capitalists, the majority of us now enter the economic process primarily as consumers. Economic agency is linked to purchasing power these days. Despite the collapse of traditional industries in recent decades, there are still those who argue that workers' associations, unions, remain the best hope for organized resistance to big business. National capitalism once made people believe in society as a place with one fixed point. But now the internet points to a more plural version of society composed of mobile networks. The mass of its ordinary users have a common interest, as individuals and pressure groups, in avoiding unreasonable regulation and retaining the economic benefits of their equal exchanges. So we may provisionally accord to the "wired" a class identity in opposition to governments and corporations.

The main players in the political economy of the internet are thus governments, corporations and the rest of us, the people (represented, let us say, by the minority who are wired). The landed interest now rests on the coercive capacity of territorial states to extract taxes and rents by right of eminent domain and on threat of punishment. Capitalist profit is concentrated in a handful of huge transnational corporations whose interest is to keep up the price of commodities and to guarantee income from property (rent) in the face of resistance to payment. Ordinary people exchange services as equals on the internet in their capacity as individuals endowed with personality and agency. The digital revolution, by radically cheapening the information attached to long-distance transactions, makes it possible for these individuals to enter several markets, notably those for credit, as persons with a known history. Governments and corporations need each other, for sure, but their interests are far from coincident. Both may be vulnerable to self-conscious use of internet resources by democratic movements aiming to subvert their respective monopolies.

The three classes of political economy

Resources	Environment	Money	Human creativity
Factors	Land	Capital	Labor
Classes then	Landlords	Capitalists	Workers
Income	Rent	Profit	Wages
Classes now	Governments	Corporations	Persons
Income	Tax / Rent	Profit / Rent	Exchange

In many ways, our world resembles the old regime of agrarian civilization and this is because unequal power has been concentrated in the hands of enforcers and rentiers. Hence the appropriateness of the term "information feudalism" for our era. The world is now witnessing the triumph of that "pseudo-aristocracy" of commercial monopolists that Jefferson once saw as the main danger to liberal democracy. It is as if the East India Company had never suffered the reverse of American independence. We could do worse, then, than return to Ricardo's focus on how wealth is distributed in human society and, in particular, on the contradiction between coercive demands for tax and rent and the formation of a world market where people in general might enjoy the benefits of the machine revolution, if they were left free to exchange goods and services as equals. Human work was once conceived of as collective physical energy, as so many "hands." The internet has raised the significance of intangible commodities. Now that production of things is being replaced to a significant degree by information services, labor is increasingly understood as individual creativity, as subjectivity. And it is this shift that has been captured by big money in the claim that "intellectual property" deserves closer regulation in the interest of its owners than it gets at present.

This is the context for current conflicts over intellectual property rights. The large corporations, in the name of the human creativity of individual authors, have launched a campaign to assert their exclusive ownership of what until recently was considered shared culture to which all had free and equal access. The "napsterization" of popular music, harbinger of peer-to-peer exchange between individual computers, is one such battle pitting the feudal barons of the music business against our common right to transmit songs as we wish. People who never knew they shared a common infrastructure of culture are now being forced to acknowledge it by aggressive policies of corporate privatization. And these policies are being promoted at the international level by the same United States government whose armed forces now seem free to run amok in the world. But others, notably the European Union, are not far behind.

In the name of protecting their intellectual property, corporate capitalists seek to impose anti-quated command and control methods on world markets whose constitutive governments have been cowed into passive compliance. The largest demonstrations against the neo-liberal world order, from Seattle to Genoa, have been mobilized to a significant degree by the need to oppose this particular version of global private property. The events of September 11th, 2001 have temporarily diminished this movement, especially in North America, just as they have added to the powers of coercion at the disposal of governments everywhere. In this sense, the global movement for greater democracy and less inequality has suffered a reverse. But the "culture war" has truly only just begun. If classical political economy's slogan of free trade was aimed at dislodging traditional feudalism, we have to get our minds around the current situation in which "free markets" and "liberal democracy" are the rhetorical disguise of feudal monopolists.

The phrase "intellectual property" seems to have been invented by Lysander Spooner. He was an old-fashioned liberal philosopher of the sort that flour-ished in the mid-nineteenth century—individualist, anarchist, abolitionist, a sort of American Proudhon. He was also frequently broke. In 1855 he published his longest work, *The Law of Intellectual Property: or an essay on the right of authors and inventors to a perpetual property in their ideas.* Spooner wanted to guarantee a living for individuals who work with their minds, claiming that copyright and patent laws were inadequate and unconstitutional. They were inadequate because they failed to protect an author's or inventor's rights in common law and unconstitutional because they deprived citizens of their property.

> Knowledge is property, and property is an inalienable and self-evident natural right. Existing laws confiscate the thinker's production and without their consent give it to others. With their property rights secured, men of intellect could then be sure of a living for their work.
>
> It is poor economy on the part of the common people to attempt by stealing... knowledge, instead of buying it, to defraud intellect of its wages. If unpaid, men of thought will serve those who will pay—oppressive governments, monopolists, armies, and other established powers; intellectuals themselves will then become agents of oppression.

Thinkers who serve the status quo—legislators, judges, lawyers, editors, teachers, doctors, soldiers—are richly rewarded, but those who serve humanity are impoverished, or worse. If the establishment frauds were replaced by a system of reward for genuine originality, the intellect could "enlighten, enrich, and liberate all mankind."

If you haven't heard of Lysander Spooner, it may be because he wanted to restrict use of his words without permission or payment. But it is more likely because the American civil war buried that libertarian moment of individual creativity and launched a new phase of corporate capitalism that has only now come to full maturity in the neo-liberal world economy. Whatever the origins of intellectual property in fifteenth century Venetian glass patents and eighteenth century author's copyright, a corporate drive is now on to privatize access to culture across the board in what has been called "the second enclosure of the commons" and its main beneficiaries are American, European and Japanese monopolists of information-based commodities. Here "culture" is taken to be an informally shared alternative to the notion that ideas can be owned as private property. It is linked to the notion of a cultural or creative commons. I wish to oppose private and common property in principle. In the first case an individual or collective entity holds exclusive rights against the world, in the second everyone has free and equal access to the resource. This latter-day enclosure movement rests in part on confusion of ordinary individuals with the highly centralized corporations whose interests drive it.

The rise of intellectual property to its current prominence as the most contested issue generated by global capitalism belongs mainly to the last two decades, but its origin lies in the late nineteenth century, when the western powers sought to consolidate their control of a world market carved up between their various empires. The Berne Convention for the Protection of Literary and Artistic Works of 1886 first established recognition of copyright between sovereign nations. Victor Hugo was its most vigorous proponent. Over a century later, in 1994, the World Trade Organization (WTO) introduced the Agreement on Trade-Related Aspects of Intellectual Property Rights (known somewhat ironically as TRIPs). This covers copyright, patents, trademarks, trade secrets, industrial designs, geographical indicia (*sic*) and integrated circuit layers. The last item reminds us that this international agreement's birth coincided with the internet going public and the invention of the World Wide Web, the launch proper of the digital revolution. The enactment of TRIPs as a mandatory feature of global trade was and is still an unprecedented attempt to make US-style intellectual property law mandatory for all countries.

The relationship of the USA to the history of international copyright is crucial. American publishers routinely ignored British copyright from the beginning and the US was slow to sign international agreements on the subject. It only joined the Berne Convention in 1989! The original signatories were Britain, France, Germany and Spain and many developing countries became members as colonies. But when the Southeast Asian "tiger" economies began their drive for modern growth in the 1960s, they did not respect international copyright, tacitly sanctioning the cheap reproduction of American textbooks that their people could not afford otherwise. With their educational expansion achieved, these "pirates," as they were labeled by the Americans, joined the Berne Convention in the 1990s. But by then the issue had shifted from books to music, movies and software; and the TRIPs treaty envisaged an altogether more comprehensive set of rules for intellectual property.

The US tried out its new recipe for globalization of intellectual property law when Ronald Reagan introduced the Caribbean Basin Economic Recovery Act in 1983. At the time the Caribbean was a hotbed of "piracy" of materials whose copyright was mainly owned in the USA. The act offered countries privileged access to the American market only if they observed the copyright of US owners. Countries like the Dominican Republic and Jamaica found that they had to introduce intellectual property laws in a hurry if they wanted to avoid exclusion from preferential tariffs. This initiative established the principle of linking trade rules to intellectual property and in the 1990s the USA entered bilateral treaties with many countries in which acceptance of the TRIPs terms was enforced by the threat of exclusion from the American market altogether. Some fifty countries also signed bilateral treaties exempting US citizens from future prosecution for war crimes, thereby bringing together the conditions for a new American empire after the millennium—military force, mercantilism and intellectual property. The European Union, without the same mix of unbridled imperialism, has followed the American lead in seeking to police intellectual property aggressively. And many of the smaller countries who vote on international regulatory bodies seem content to go along with this policy. Only the larger non-western countries, such as Brazil, India, China and South Africa, have so far resisted; and even they are not immune to trade pressure, as the recent Indian patents law, restricting the production of cheap generic drugs to the benefit of the western pharmaceutical monopolies, has shown.

The first sector of information goods to feel the full implications of the digital revolution has been recorded music. Many people feel that the feudal barons, led by the Recording Industry Association of America (RIAA), have already lost the war against free peer-to-peer exchange of music files. Record sales have slumped dramatically and the attempt to haul a random assortment of offenders into the courts of the USA, Britain and France is unlikely to stem the tide in the long run. The movie industry is at a more critical stage. Here the age of cheap reproduction has generated huge revenues to the main studios from sales of video or DVD copies in addition to cinema seats and the Moving Pictures Association (MPA) has been a leader of the drive to fight "piracy," which is out of control in the countries of the former Soviet empire and Asia. This campaign is not just legal, but technical, with the machines being modified to prevent use across patented standards or borders and hackers circumventing these restrictions as they arise. The contrast with a century ago is instructive. Then filmmakers went West to Hollywood in an attempt to escape the restrictions of Edison's East Coast monopoly. Pioneers like Walt Disney exemplified the frontier mentality of the industry at that time, lifting much of his first Mickey Mouse cartoon from a Buster Keaton movie without attribution. Now the Disney Corporation engages in litigation around the world to protect its private ownership of images and slogans that would not have been covered by copyright without recent legislation.

Because of its centrality to the digital revolution, the market for software is crucial to the struggle over intellectual property. Software consists of disembodied machines, recipes of pure information that achieve their effects through a variety of material forms (hardware). Since reproduction of these recipes is virtually costless, their ownership as commodities poses an acute problem for any corporate strategy of accumulation. Even so, the Microsoft Corporation has built a position of market dominance for its Windows system by licensing software whose source code is kept secret from the public. A movement has arisen to challenge this commercial monopoly, Free/Libre/Open Source Software (FLOSS), which is itself divided between those who oppose selling as such and those who accept money payment as long as users have access to the source code and can modify and reproduce it with acknowledgment. These initiatives accept the need for legal protection though such instruments as the General Public License (GPL) and the Creative Commons license introduced by Stanford law professor, Lawrence Lessig, who for many now symbolizes the movement to end commercial monopoly that started with hackers like MIT's Richard Stallman and the Finnish boy wonder, Linus Torvalds.

FLOSS has one great advantage over the monopolists. It can pool the talents of tens of thousands of software engineers, both amateur and professional, whereas Microsoft can hire only a few workers and relies on its customers to discover problems through trial and error. Moreover, its licenses are less restrictive and this has made the most widely used system of open source software, Linux, attractive to some of the leading corporations in the computing industry. IBM has now embraced Linux and is helping Lula's Brazilian government to convert the public sector to open source software. Microsoft's business methods are notoriously predatory, as in the browser war with Netscape that led to some anti-trust wrist-slapping within the USA. Despite the current market share of the USA, the diffusion of the digital revolution around the world is faster than for any previous communications technology. Already Hewlett-Packard, for example, are targeting the four billion poorest inhabitants of the world, which means setting up test sites in China, the Middle East and Africa to find out how machinery and software have to be modified for conditions there.

Perhaps the critical player in this fast-evolving scenario is India, with its vast population and huge pool of cheap, computer-literate English-speakers, not to mention a diaspora that is steadily returning home from Silicon Valley. The relocation of global information services to cities like Bangalore, Hyderabad and Mumbai has already invoked the specter of massive middle-class job loss for the western media. But of equal significance is the current process whereby thousands of decisions are being made at every level of government and society to install the software and machines that will establish Indian standards for decades to come. The main competitors are Microsoft and Linux (promoted by its own commercial corporations such as Red Hat Linux). The latter promote their software by stressing that it is cheaper, more robust and flexible than Windows. Bill Gates, on the other hand, emphasizes Microsoft's track record of collaboration with government bureaucracy in regulating access to the internet.

This is the nub of the intellectual property issue. As in the case of the East India Company's tea monopoly, a few huge corporations rely on the laws and policing powers of venal governments to maintain artificially high profits and rents. The US Congress has shown itself to be willing to invent and extend intellectual property rights designed to benefit these corporations in fields stretching from entertainment to the chemical industry. A powerful system of legal enforcement at home, when combined with world market share and American insularity, has led some to assume that the USA can impose its own solutions to the commercial challenge of the digital revolution. This strategy has now gone global through international treaties such as TRIPs and the saber-rattling we have come to expect from the world's sole remaining superpower. But, just as Edison's monopoly was once circumvented by Hollywood, the contemporary shift of economic power to Asia exposes the cracks in this American bid for empire.

It is American corporations and American activists that have so far led the opposition to the monopolists; and their liberal constitution still exercises a powerful grip over American minds, even if some corporations want to reinvent the East India Company and the President thinks he is George II. Recently, Richard Stallman dug up an internal memo from Bill Gates in 1991:

> If people had understood how patents would be granted when most of today's ideas were invented and had taken out patents, the industry would be at a complete standstill today… A future start-up with no patents of its own will be forced to pay whatever price the giants choose to impose.

Now Gates calls detractors of intellectual property rules "communists." It's an old story, the dynamism of small entrepreneurs versus monopolies protected by state power. Maybe we need another liberal revolution against the fake freedoms of George I's "new world order." But the political contours of such a revolution are hard to imagine at present.

The fundamental weakness of the "neo-liberal" (read "mercantilist") attempt to build a "free" world market on the principles of command and control is that its very means of self-propagation, the digital revolution, promotes a broader conception of democracy than the alliance of governments and corporations is likely to be able to contain. We have been here before, of course, through writers such as Marx and Veblen, who likewise argued for the inherently progressive nature of the machine revolution. But then society was being centralized at all levels and now, just possibly, it is not. Taking the argument to the level of global political economy has inevitably pushed the hit man's dilemma out of sight. It is hard to represent social change on this scale in terms of the personal judgments reached by ordinary human beings. Yet the struggle to shape the future of digital production and exchange is substantially a moral one. Businessmen, politicians and the lawyers who defend them are often accused of immorality, lying and even of committing crimes. Public bureaucracies are said to be indifferent to human interests. The legions of activists who make up the movement for democracy from below are likewise motivated by an ethical politics in which personal responsibility will count for more than it does at present.

The history of private property contains both sides of the hit man's dilemma, personal agency and its impersonal conditions, but the difference between them has been elided. This has allowed the rhetoric and symbolism of the liberal revolutions to be appropriated by powerful interests whose aim is the opposite of democracy. And world society now resembles the old regime as a result. The debate surrounding intellectual property is a major example of this. Copyright was intended originally in the eighteenth century to protect the interests of individual authors and their interests are routinely invoked today to justify the extraction of rent by a handful of corporations running the music, movie and software businesses. My essay has tried to show how the liberal project turned into its contemporary antithesis. I would like to use classical liberalism to sustain a critique of what passes for neo-liberalism today. At the very least this might drive a wedge between the apologists for this new enclosure of the commons and the ideology they routinely invoke to disguise their real purposes. I hold that there was some value in the modern attempt to carve out a sphere of impersonal social life; but the result has been to drive individuality, moral purpose and even religion from the conduct of our common affairs. In the face of creeping corporate totalitarianism, we need to be able to separate the personal and impersonal dimensions of our associational life in order to combine them in new ways. One way of doing that it is to take the question of intellectual property to the level of the individual human actors we know of as "intellectuals," even if it is a pejorative term in Anglophone societies. This in turn entails a brief discussion of the fate of their normal habitat, the universities, in the age of corporate privatization.

The Crisis of the Intellectuals Revisited

I recounted earlier the episode when Kant's cosmopolitan morality was overthrown in court by Hegel's political philosophy. Hegel put it all together in *The Philosophy of Right* (1821) which both contains the intellectual agendas of the giants of modern social theory—Marx, Weber, and Durkheim—and provided the blueprint for the social form that has dominated our world for a century and a half. I call this form "national capitalism," the attempt to reap the economic benefits of capitalism and moderate its socially harmful effects through central bureaucracy. There is a lot to be said for the intellectual integrity of Hegel's proposals, but they constitute in effect a counter-revolution against the liberal revolution. The chief consequence of this counter-revolution was the merger between states and corporations that has culminated in the neo-liberal world economy of our day. The universities have been around in some form for many centuries, but they only came into their own in the second half of the twentieth century, as the training grounds for bureaucracy that Hegel envisaged. Most contemporary intellectuals have taken refuge in them by now and human personality has been in retreat there for some time, appearing only sporadically like a ghost at twilight.

In *Enemies of Promise: publishing, perishing and the eclipse of scholarship*, Lindsay Waters, humanities editor for Harvard University Press, claims that the current explosion of academic publishing is a bubble as certain to burst as the dot com boom. His essay is a warning to academics, in the face of the corporate takeover of the university,

> ...to preserve and protect the independence of their activities, before the market becomes our prison and the value of the book becomes undermined.... We scholars and publishers have allowed the moneychangers into the temple. We need to restrict their activities, because we cannot kick them out the way Jesus did (since) many universities are, in significant part, financial holding operations.... The commercialization of higher education has caused innovation in the humanities to come to a standstill.

Publishing, he says, has become more concerned with quantity than quality and "the drive to mechanize the university has proved lethal over the last three decades." To save the book from the onslaught of money and machines, "we must get back to square one—by asking why anyone would want to speak, write or publish in the first place."

Waters' jeremiad for the humanities is based on sound evidence, but his analysis of the reasons for their decline puts the blame on money and machines, so that his call for resistance to university administrations has no practical basis in contemporary social and technical conditions. Getting "back to square one" is not usually a viable option for most of us. If we want to promote humanism, we should ask what historical conditions make our initiative possible and why we in particular might succeed. "Socialism" is passé these days because social democracy threw out money and markets when it rejected liberal democracy. Maybe we should concentrate on the goal of democracy without worrying about whether it is liberal or social. This essay has begun to sketch some of the history and analysis that might make such a goal more feasible than it often seems now.

In 1993 Anna Grimshaw and I published a pamphlet, *Anthropology and the Crisis of the Intellectuals*, to launch Prickly Paradigm's precursor imprint. We tried to locate anthropology's compromised relationship to academic bureaucracy in the crisis facing modern intellectuals, as identified by C.L.R. James in *American Civilization*. We were barely aware of the internet going public in the same year nor of its imminent transformation by the World Wide Web. We held that intellectual practice should be integrated more closely with social life, given their increasing separation by academic bureaucracy. This escape from the ivory tower to join the people where they live was the inspiration for modern anthropology. But it had been negated by the expansion of the universities after 1945 and by the political pressures exerted on British academics in particular since the 1980s.

Edward Said, in *The Intellectual as Exile*, his BBC Reith lectures of 1992, without ever mentioning anthropology, made claims for intellectuals that could be taken as a metaphor for the discipline. He emphasized the creative possibilities in migration and marginality, of being an awkward outsider who crosses boundaries, questions certainties, a figure at once involved and detached. Narrow professionalism poses an immense threat to academic life. Specialization, concern with disciplinary boundaries and expert knowledge lead to a suspension of critical enquiry and ultimately a drift towards legitimating power. The exile and the amateur might combine to inject new radicalism into a jaded professionalism. Said credited James with being an intellectual of the kind he advocated, but James placed intellectuals within the contradictions of modern society, in a historical process that had aligned them with power and made them increasingly at odds with the people. Said generalized from his own personal trajectory, but his blind spot was politics. He failed to identify the political forces that had transformed intellectual life from being free individual creativity into serving the specialized needs of bureaucracy. The issue, now that the Cold War had recently ended, was whether those intellectuals who chose to reject bureaucratic conformity would have significant social forces at their back or would be condemned to fruitless isolation. This issue takes on a new resonance after September 11th.

For James there was a growing conflict between the concentration of power at the top of society and the aspirations of people everywhere for democracy to be extended into all areas of their lives. This conflict was most advanced in America. The struggle was for civilization or barbarism, for individual freedom within new and expanded conceptions of social life (democracy) or a fragmented and repressed subjectivity stifled by coercive bureaucracies (totalitarianism). The intellectuals were caught between the expansion of bureaucracy and the growing power and presence of people as a force in world society. Unable to recognize that people's lives mattered more than their own ideas, they oscillated between an introspective individualism (psychoanalysis) and service to the ruling powers, whether of the right (fascism) or left (Stalinism). As a result, the traditional role of the intellectual as an independent witness and critic standing unequivocally for truth had been seriously compromised. The absorption of the bulk of intellectuals as wage slaves and pensioners of bureaucracy not only removed their independence but separated their specialized activities from social life.

One anthropologist who addressed these questions of intellectuals and the public, of ideas and life, knowledge and power, was Edmund Leach in his prescient BBC Reith lectures of 1967, *A Runaway World?* There he identified a world in movement, marked by the interconnectedness of people and things. This provoked the mood of optimism and fear that characterized the sixties, when established structures seemed to be breaking down. The reality of change could not be understood through conventional cultural categories predicated on stable order. Moral categories based on habits of separation and division could only make the world's movement seem alien and frightening. An ethos of scientific detachment reinforced by binary ideas (right/wrong) lay at the core of society's malaise. Leach called for an intellectual practice based on movement and engagement, connection and dialectic. In short he was calling for the reinsertion of ideas into life.

The solution to our problems cannot be found in increased specialization, in the discovery of new areas of social life to colonize with the aid of old professional paradigms or a return to literary scholarship disguised as a new dialogical form. It requires new patterns of social engagement extending beyond the universities to the widest reaches of world society. This in turn depends on placing ourselves in a position first of acknowledging how people everywhere are pushing back the boundaries of the old society and second of being open to universality, most versions of which have been driven underground by national capitalism and would be buried forever if the present corporate privatization of the cultural commons as intellectual property is allowed to succeed.

The academic tradition has been one of open access to published information with full citation of sources, allowing readers to follow the scholar's tracks for their own purposes. The Open Source software movement is based on similar principles. Individual competition for the glory of discovery has usually been moderated in academia by a culture of informal sharing that takes in teacher-student interaction, seminars, conferences and collegial relations. The recent expansion of academic bureaucracy has accentuated the objectification of thought as a marker of status and reward. Ideas have become commodities to be possessed individually, traded and stolen. The current panic over plagiarism, especially by students, is one result of the contradiction between exclusive private property and a human conversation now reproduced digitally. An intensified focus on the formal abstraction of performance has led to the academic labor market being driven by the empty measures of print production that Lindsay Waters rightly denigrates. Subjective contributions, such as the qualities that mark a good teacher, inevitably carry much less weight.

And so the academic intellectuals, who might have offered a critique of the corporate takeover of the universities, find themselves instead drawn into a vicious variant of the privatization of ideas. In the process, much that was valuable in academic life has been lost. The university is already looking like an endangered species of institution as a result. Perhaps it was too closely yoked to that alliance between governments and corporations that drove national capitalism in its heyday. Universities may survive the social forces transforming the contemporary world in name and material form, but the content of what goes on within them will soon be unrecognizable as that medieval guild tradition that the twentieth century made its own.

I endorse Lindsay Waters' call for a humanist revival. Something must be done to reinstate human personality in our common understanding of how the world works. But this should be through the medium of money, markets and machines, not despite them. Friedrich Engels once wrote a polemic against the likes of William Morris called *Socialism, Utopian and Scientific*. Socialists were "utopian" when their slogan was "stop the world, I want to get off," when they dreamed of escaping from industrial capitalism into an earlier, simpler age. They were "scientific" when, like the Marxists, they aspired to understand contemporary economic history and take it in a more democratic direction. Then, as now, society was becoming coordinated more rapidly and effectively at the top than the bottom. In my recent book on money, my first idea was that the cheapening of information transfers as a result of the digital revolution might allow the impersonal economy of the twentieth century to be "repersonalized," by attaching more information to individual transactions and potentially granting individuals greater control over work, consumption and credit. But it did not take me long to realize that a fully personal economy would return us all to the world of gangsters, both medieval and modern. We need new impersonal norms capable of standardizing social interactions where the nation-state can no longer reach—law, money, education, technology—the list is endless. So our task is not to replace impersonal society with personal life, but to discover new ways of combining them.

The hit man's dilemma is to be human or inhuman. It is a dilemma shared by kings, generals, presidents and CEOs, when they contemplate the human cost of an action undertaken on behalf of some collective interest. It probably won't go away. But I have argued in this essay that our ability to devise ways of curbing the high-handed behavior of the powerful has been deeply undermined by a legal culture that grants business corporations the rights of living persons. The liberal revolutions against the old regime—especially, in view of later developments, the American war of independence—sought to guarantee citizens equal (and therefore impersonal) rights in society. This meant being very clear about the difference between individual persons and impersonal institutions. Such a separation was intrinsic to the rise of modern capitalism, as we have seen. But capitalism took a bureaucratic turn in the late nineteenth century and this was the time that business corporations, beginning in the USA, sought to collapse the distinction between real and artificial persons in economic law. The impersonal society of the twentieth century flourished on this basis and, for many people, the idea that they might exercise personal responsibility in the economic or political spheres became simply inconceivable. Some intellectuals jumped onto the obvious corruption of liberal ideals to advocate a variety of anti-liberal ideologies, drawing on the same confusion of people, ideas and things that had become normal in law and even in ordinary language.

At the beginning of this century, we have grown familiar with the spectacle of strong states and sometimes even stronger transnational corporations riding roughshod over human rights and international law itself in the name of the "free market," especially for digital commodities. The struggle to reverse this "information feudalism" must take place at many different levels. Here I have argued that one of them should be to re-examine the metaphysics of where personal agency meets the impersonal conditions of its expression. We might begin by making such an enquiry explicitly historical. For the confusion of our times is fed by an indifference to history that allows the heirs of America's anti-colonial revolution to reinvent the corporate monopolies of absolutist monarchy in the name of liberal democracy. If the Europeans can't see through this, perhaps the Chinese, Indians or Brazilians will. We cannot return to the eighteenth century, but we can learn how we got from there to here, rather than remain trapped in the timeless generalizations of ideology.

In the spirit of John Locke, we must confront the semantic criminals who pollute our public discourse with their dissembling words. These are the hired spokesmen of the economic criminals who aim to hijack the machine revolution for their own immoral ends. George Orwell, where are you when we most need you? As for the notion that there is a difference between the operational standards of legal and illegal businesses, well, nobody believes that any more, do they? A book in the amazon.com top hundred as I write draws an explicit parallel between the central metaphor of this essay and normal business. According to its blurb,

John Perkins, a former chief economist at Boston strategic-consulting firm Chas. T. Main, says he was an "economic hit man" for 10 years, helping U.S. intelligence agencies and multinationals cajole and blackmail foreign leaders into serving U.S. foreign policy and awarding lucrative contracts to American business. "Economic hit men (EHMs) are highly paid professionals who cheat countries around the globe out of trillions of dollars," Perkins writes. *Confessions of an Economic Hit Man* is an extraordinary and gripping tale of intrigue and dark machinations. Think John Le Carré, except it's a true story.

The wild banking boom of the nineties produced similar confessions of murderous mayhem in firms like Morgan Stanley that make *The Sopranos* look like the comedy of manners it really is:

Frank Partnoy takes us to the annual drunken skeet-shooting competition, FIASCO, where he and his colleagues sharpen the killer instincts they are encouraged to use against their competitors, their clients, and each other.

Yet at the same time a huge propaganda effort seeks to persuade us to accept plutocracy as the only way that society can serve the common interest. Perhaps it takes a Nixon to explode this doublethink, to show us that capitalism's moral economy, resting as it does on the division of human experience into personal and impersonal spheres, where objective power is not made humanly accountable, is a dangerous illusion.

Conclusions

The formal conclusions of this essay are consistent with the late Durkheim of *The Elementary Forms of the Religious Life*. Every human being is a unique person who lives in society. We are therefore all individual and social at the same time and the two are inseparable in our experience. Society is both inside and outside us; and a lot rides on our ability to tell the difference as well as to make a meaningful connection between them. Society is personal when it is lived by each of us in particular; it is impersonal when it takes the form of collective ideas. Life and ideas are likewise inseparable in practice, but they need sometimes to be distinguished.

It is therefore just as damaging to insist on a radical separation of individuals and society or of life and ideas as it is to collapse the difference between them. We have seen that modern capitalism rests on a division between personal and impersonal spheres of social life. The institution of private property initially drove a conceptual wedge between our individuality and an active sense of belonging to society. Indeed the latter was made invisible or at least unreachable for most of us. But then private property assumed the form of public ownership by large business corporations and even governments. It then became convenient to merge the personal and impersonal spheres in economic law, leaving a general confusion in political culture between the rights of individual citizens and those of abstract social entities wielding far more power than any human being ever could. The consequences for democracy are disastrous.

Is it so hard to distinguish between real persons and the impersonal organizations they live by? Bill Gates is Bill Gates, not Microsoft, and, when he plays bridge with Warren Buffet, they talk about money, with consequences for the rest of us. We have no difficulty with a play that represents modern physics as a meeting between Nils Bohr and Werner Heisenberg in Copenhagen. The problem is that even the academic humanities have become so abstract that it has become quaintly old-fashioned to imagine that living people are what make society and ideas. The Anglophone founders of classical liberalism from Locke to Smith and Jefferson knew that and their greatest poets, from Milton to Blake, expressed it in words whose meaning we have forgotten. "General Forms have their vitality in Particulars, and every Particular is a Man."

Max Weber has been a constant companion on this journey. Writing a century ago, in the full spate of a bureaucratic revolution powered by machine industry, Weber saw no social force capable of resisting a highly centralized version of impersonal society. Our perspective, looking back at the twentieth century, is rather different. On the one hand, bureaucratic capitalism has evolved to a highly mobile form operating on a global scale; on the other, national bureaucracy sometimes seems to be an endangered species and its industrial basis in the old centers of western power has almost withered away, only to be reborn in Asia. Before public bureaucracy is finally killed off, we need to reflect on how the hopes it once embodied might be preserved, if for no other reason than to offer an institutional alternative to the transnational corporations now setting the rules for world economy. If I have been critical of corporate monopolists here, I still believe that some economic functions can only be performed by corporations of a certain size and that capitalism's historical mission to bring cheap commodities to the human masses is still far from complete. So there is room for more progressive capitalist firms to take a leading part in dismantling the resuscitated old regime that calls itself "neo-liberalism."

The latest stage of the machine revolution, the convergence of telephones, television and computers in a digital network of communications, has speeded up human connection at the world level. Society now takes a number of forms—global, regional, national and local. We need new impersonal norms to guide our social interactions in such a world, but not if it means denying the significance of individual personalities. The stage is set for a new humanism capable of uniting these poles of our existence. The word "humanity" contains within itself the elements of our predicament and their potential synthesis. It is a collective noun, a moral quality and a historical project for our species. If it is not obvious to us now how these make up our common humanity, then that is because we have just stumbled into a machine revolution whose implications we can barely imagine. We are still primitives; but eventually we, the people, will make society on our own terms, if we master the means of its development, machines and money. In the course of doing so, we will encounter immense social forces bent on denying the drive for a genuine democracy. My essay has aimed to clarify who the sides and what the stakes are in this struggle for world society.

But there is more to it than class war. Somehow, in the last decade or two, the idea of government has been replaced by public talk of "governance." The chief reason for this is to acknowledge that responsibility for maintaining social order has shifted from the nation-state's monopoly to a more diffuse pattern of regulation located at many levels of world society in a variety of corporate institutions inside and outside government of the conventional sort. Even more recently, this talk has taken a distinctly ethical shift to a focus on "good governance." There is little doubt that "good" here means moral behavior on the part of persons holding office and it contains an explicit appeal for popular support on grounds that go beyond the legal rationality of traditional bureaucracy. We could say that it constitutes a revival of Durkheim's agenda as a solution to Weber's gloomy prognosis. This could be dismissed as a cynical disguise of power, as the usual manipulation of a gullible public by a transnational oligarchy. But I believe that it speaks to a genuine desire to fill the gap between politics and morality left by the twentieth-century experiment in impersonal society. In this respect, the remarkable strength of religious feeling in the world's most modern society, when taken with the ability of Islam to articulate resistance to America's global domination, is not an anomalous hangover from the past, but rather evidence of a widespread desire for meaningful connection in a world where the secular state's grip on society has been weakened. It was never strong in the USA to start with.

Modern knowledge, as organized by the universities, falls into three broad classes: the natural sciences, the social sciences and the humanities. This is to say that the academic division of labor in our day is concerned with nature, society and humanity, of which the first two are thought to be governed by objective laws, but knowledge of the last requires the exercise of subjectivity or critical judgment. Whereas nature and society may be known by means of impersonal disciplines, human experience is communicated between persons, between individual artists and their audiences. Nature and humanity are represented conventionally through science and art, but the best way of approaching society is moot, since social science is a recent (and, in my view, failed) attempt to bring the methods of the natural sciences to bear on a task that previously had fallen to religion. If science is the commitment to know the world objectively and art the means of expressing oneself subjectively, religion was and is a bridge between subject and object, a way of making meaningful connection between something inside oneself and the world outside. For a time it seemed that science had driven religion from the government of modern societies, but the search is on now for new forms of religion capable of reconciling scientific laws with personal experience. Kant's cosmopolitan moral politics offer one vision of the course such a religious renewal might take. It turns out that the hit man's dilemma is one way of talking about a general human crisis. ■

Acknowledgments

I am very pleased that Marshall Sahlins and Matthew Engelke gave me this chance to revisit the pamphlet form in their impressive successor to the series that Anna Grimshaw and I started. The essay draws on my network of friends, colleagues and students in all sorts of intangible ways. But special thanks go to Felix Stalder, Sandy Robertson, Jeff Morrow, Knut Nustad and Galina Lindquist for their comments on a late draft. Shekhar Krishnan tried to get me to address a younger Asian audience for this piece. Sophie Chevalier had to put up with my angst when the text refused to come and my withdrawal when it did. *The Hit Man's Dilemma* is dedicated to the magical twins, my daughters, born on the same day 28 years apart. Perhaps the world they help to make will not be as hung up on the fruitless opposition between morality and politics as mine has been.

Paris, Easter 2005

Further Reading

Abbott, Jennifer and Mark Achbar. *The Corporation.* *(Three-part Documentary, 2003)*
  http://www.imdb.com/title/tt0379225/

The American Heritage Dictionary of the English Language. (Third Edition, Houghton Mifflin, 1996)

Avineri, Shlomo. *Hegel's Theory of the Modern State.* (Cambridge UP, 1972)

Caffentzis, George. *Clipped Coins, Abused Words and Civil Government: John Locke's philosophy of money.* (Autonomedia, 1989)

Drahos, Peter. *Information Feudalism: who owns the knowledge economy?* (Earthscan, 2002)

Durkheim, Emile. *The Elementary Forms of the Religious Life* (Free Press, 1965 [1912])

Grimshaw, Anna and Keith Hart. *Anthropology and the Crisis of the Intellectuals.* (Prickly Pear, 1993)

Hart, Keith. *Money in an Unequal World: Keith Hart and his memory bank.* (Texere, 2001)

Hartmann, Thom. *Unequal Protection: the rise of corporate dominance and the theft of human rights.* (Rodale, 2002)

Heidegger, Martin. *The Fundamental Concepts of Metaphysics: world, finitude, solitude.* (Indiana UP, 1983 [1930])

Hicks, Sir John. *A Theory of Economic History.* (Oxford UP, 1969)

James, C.L.R. *American Civilization.* (Blackwell, 1993)

Kant, Immanuel. *Perpetual Peace: a philosophical sketch.* (Internet, 1795)

Leach, Edmund. *A Runaway World?* (BBC, 1968)

Lessig, Lawrence. *Free Culture: how big media uses technology and the law to lock down culture and control creativity.* (Penguin, 2004)

Macpherson, C.B. (editor). *Property: mainstream and critical positions.* (University of Toronto, 1978)

Marx, Karl. *Capital: the critique of political economy Volume 1.* (Lawrence & Wishart, 1970 [1867])

Mehta, Suketu. *Maximum City: Bombay lost and found.* (Alfred Knopf, 2005)

Naughton, John. *A Brief History of the Future: the origins of the internet.* (Weidenfeld & Nicholson, 1999)

Partnoy, Frank. *F.I.A.S.C.O.: the inside story of a Wall Street trader.* (Penguin, 1999)

Perkins, John. *Confessions of an Economic Hit Man.* (Berrett-Koehler, 2004)

Rousseau, Jean-Jacques. *Discourse on Inequality.* (Penguin, 1984 [1754])

Shell, Marc. *The Economy of Literature.* (Johns Hopkins UP, 1978)

Simmel, Georg. "The metropolis and mental life." *The Sociology of Georg Simmel.* ed. by Kurt Wolff. (Free Press, 1950)

Simmel, Georg. *The Philosophy of Money.* (Routledge, 1978 [1900])

Soley, Lawrence. *Leasing the Ivory Tower: the corporate takeover of academia.* (South End, 1995)

Weber, Max. "The city: on non-legitimate domination." *Economy and Society.* ed. by Roth & Wittich. (University of California, 1978, volume 2)

Visit www.thememorybank.co.uk for more work, published and unpublished, by Keith Hart.

Also available from Prickly Paradigm Press: